THE CASE AGAINST VOTING REFORM

THE CASE AGAINST VOTING REFORM: WHY THE AV SYSTEM WOULD DAMAGE BRITAIN

James Forder

ONEWORLD

OXFORD

A Oneworld Book

Published by Oneworld Publications 2011

Copyright © James Forder 2011

The moral right of James Forder to be identified as the
Author of this work has been asserted by him in accordance
with the Copyright, Designs and Patents Act 1988

ISBN:978–1–85168–825–8

Typeset by Jayvee, Trivandrum, India
Cover design by Leo Nickolls
Printed and bound in Great Britain by Page Bros, Norwich

Oneworld Publications
185 Banbury Road
Oxford OX2 7AR
England

Learn more about Oneworld. Join our mailing list to
find out about our latest titles and special offers at:

www.oneworld-publications.com

CONTENTS

INTRODUCTION

The coalition government has decided that forty-five million British people will have the opportunity to decide whether we should change our voting system. It is the most important decision we have faced for decades because the proposed reform threatens to wreck our democracy.

The proposal that we adopt the so-called 'alternative vote' seems to be one that practically no one, including many of those campaigning for it, actually supports. Many people support 'proportional representation' but the alternative vote is not such a system. On this point, the Liberal Democrat leader Nick Clegg gave the game away before the 2010 election, when he called the alternative vote 'a miserable little compromise'.[1]

Rather than being advocated for its own characteristics,

support for the alternative vote seems to flow from the idea that it is some sort of movement towards proportional representation. But the two are really very different.

Under the alternative vote, voters have the option of ranking the candidates as their first, second and third choices (and so on). Initially, the number of first preferences for each candidate is counted. If any one has more than half, he or she is elected. If not, the bottom candidate is eliminated. The votes for that candidate are then reallocated according to the second preferences of the voters. A candidate with more than half the votes at this stage is elected. If no one has half the votes, the bottom candidate is eliminated again and the process continues until someone has more than half the votes. That person is the winner. Under such a system, the House of Commons would be made up of the winners from each constituency (as it is at present). In contrast, systems of proportional representation aim at achieving a close relationship between the proportion of votes for each party and the proportion of seats it takes in Parliament. The alternative vote offers no pretence of achieving that. Some people, however, seem to think that whatever the limitations of the alternative vote, it is a bit more like a proportional system than our current one. Even that is only true in some situations, but more of its supporters, I suspect, have the idea that if they can win a referendum on it, circumstances will soon enough arise in which we can have another vote on another system.

INTRODUCTION

The trouble is that the ultimate aim of the process – proportional representation – is itself greatly misunderstood. As the debate has been conducted in Britain, not even its opponents have made the best case against it. Even more notably, many of its supporters give the impression of having no idea that there might be even a reasonable basis for opposing it. And far too much argument is wasted on questions of detail about the advantages and disadvantages of various systems of proportional representation, of which there are literally hundreds. There are plenty of guides to the various systems which discuss these details,[2] but the point of this book is rather different – it is to dismiss the principle of proportionality.

My central message is that proportional representation is a *menace* to effective democracy and if the alternative vote is a movement towards it, then it is a menace as well. In addition, whatever else it does, the alternative vote certainly brings its own distinctive disadvantages. And just because it is not a proportional system does not mean it avoids the disadvantages of systems that are. The upshot is that whilst there is no denying that it is miserable, it is not really true that it is a compromise. It offers a fine example of the worst of all worlds. There should be no doubt of the necessity of a 'no' vote in the referendum.

As the argument over proportional representation is usually conducted, the most important point its advocates make is that the current system is 'unfair' because it does not generally result in the proportion of MPs of each party being the same as the proportion of votes cast for them across the country. It is even possible for one party to have more MPs than another despite having fewer votes. In a couple of very close elections since 1945, this has actually happened but much more frequently it delivers results that leave the smaller parties under-represented relative to the proportion of votes they receive. It is true that various other systems can offer better approximations to proportionality in Parliament than the present system. However, in most cases they are only better approximations – when it comes to the details, the advocates of proportional representation shy away from systems that would actually deliver the greatest possible proportionality. Nevertheless, again and again, the crucial point alleged to make the case for proportional representation turns on this principle of it being 'fair' and hence 'more democratic'.

Against this, the opponents of reform make two points. One concerns the relationship between MPs and their constituents. None of the proportional systems makes every MP the only member elected to represent their constituency; some have multi-member constituencies and others have some MPs with no constituencies at all. Whether the loss of the single-member constituency would be a price worth paying, if there were a worthwhile improvement on offer,

I am not sure. There may be advantages in making a single person responsible for representing certain electors and there certainly are in avoiding having two classes of MPs. However, we might suspect that some MPs think themselves rather more important to their constituents than they really are. Most people, after all, do not know so much as their MP's name. The second point is that reform would make hung parliaments – that is, parliaments in which no party has a majority – almost inevitable. The consequence would be that coalition government would become the norm and, it is said, coalitions tend to be unstable and weak. There is certainly something in that argument but equally, the advocates of reform have had no difficulty in pointing to countries such as Germany, in which coalitions have been stable and seem to have offered satisfactory government.

To these major points both sides add other, subsidiary, ones. Among the reformists, it has been widely claimed that certain versions of proportional representation would make MPs more independent of their parties and that it would make the conduct of politics generally more co-operative and less confrontational. On the question of individual independence, it is interesting that the opponents of reform also argue that the current system – since it gives a certain amount of power of selection to local organisations – allows MPs who retain local support to be considerably independent of their party hierarchy. There does not seem to be much in the way of real evidence on the issue of whether reform would make politics more collaborative and less antagonistic. A more important point – which will feature prominently in what follows – is whether it would be desirable if it did.

It is also said that the current system often generates large changes in parliamentary representation from small changes in voting patterns. This point was greatly emphasised by the advocates of proportional representation in the 1970s, particularly following the work of Samuel Finer, who found in it an explanation of frequent changes of government, which he thought damaging.[3] His work was overtaken by events when four elections in a row were won by the Conservatives and then three by Labour but this point still seems to influence opinion in reformist circles. Another idea is that proportional systems promote the election of women and candidates from ethnic minorities, although the evidence for this cannot be described as better than mixed. And of course there is a miscellany of other points, which are very often really only rehashes of these.

Most of the time, these ideas are treated as adornments of their case even by those who advance them. The crucial ground – which is nearly always regarded as decisive by both sides – lies between the claims of a 'fairer' or 'more democratic' system and those of strong or stable government. In this form, the argument is rehearsed again and again up and down the country by partisans well-practised in move and counter-move.

One example of the kind of argument that has become rather routine comes from the 'Independent Commission on the Voting System' (usually known as the 'Jenkins Commission', after its Liberal Democrat chairman).[4] This group was set up near the beginning of the Blair government, ostensibly to make a recommendation on which of the many systems of proportional representation might be the best candidate to replace the current system. In fact, the Commission rehearsed the arguments for proportional representation in general, offered their thoughts on various possibilities and finally recommended a system of their own devising. Nothing was done about it because the government lost interest in the question. Although there is little in the report that had not been widely discussed in previous years, it offers a useful reference, simply because it is so conventional in its treatment of so many of the issues and so displays many of the problems with the reformists' case.

My argument, in contrast, is that when attention is focussed on the details of the various systems – as it usually is – it misses all the important points. The reformists, in particular, simply start in the wrong place. Rather than just making a quick calculation about whether each party has a proportional number of seats in the House of Commons and if not, declaring the result 'unfair', we should begin by asking what the *purpose* of elections is. To give a reasonable answer to that, we need to begin with an enquiry into the nature and idea of democracy.

When we do that, two things become apparent. First, there are different conceptions of democracy, embodying different ideas of what it seeks to achieve and what is valuable about it, and hence leading to different ideas about how to secure its benefits. There is nothing that we might call a pure and perfect 'democracy' and consequently nothing much to be said about whether one more or less democratic system is closer to perfection than another. Second, on any conception, democracy is a very limited system – even at its best, it cannot achieve as much as many seem to hope. That is not to suggest that there is a better system but rather to say that it is easy to expect too much of it. Certainly it is essential to remember that what we need is a system that actually works to deliver those very important benefits that are available from democracy. We do not need some idealists' system, based on a dream of a democracy either lost in Anglo-Saxon England, or yet to be discovered in the constitution of a New Jerusalem, but which does not work.

When considering the design of effective democracy, the first essential is to recognise that we must be ruthlessly realistic about the actual operation of democracies. In particular, we must accept that the central objective of politics is the seeking of power. Surely, politicians also have public-spirited and principled motivations, and if not, it costs us nothing to pay them the courtesy of pretending they have. What is inescapable, though, is that the competition for power is intense and it is not often won by those who are less than fully committed to the contest. Those who do not have the egos and the hunger for power to match their competitors do not rise to positions of leadership. Those who are keen to give their opponents credit where it is due and to admit the limitations of their own ideas are not those who win. Much the same applies to political parties. If it is an exaggeration to say that they are *merely* organisations which exist for the purpose of promoting their leaders into positions of power, it is *only* an exaggeration. If they do not perform that role – and perform it with energy and determination – their leaders go nowhere and the parties fade away.

Party loyalists, of course, will not like that view. For them, it is the leaders of other parties who are power-crazed and selfish, in hock to vested interests and happy to lie about their plans for government. For them, their own party's policies – change though they do from election to election – serve the national interest; others' are just foolishness and deception. An excellent and pertinent example is the issue of the voting system itself. We all know that some parties stand to gain electorally from reform and some to lose and that party loyalists' pattern of support or opposition for voting change has a certain, shall we say, correlation with the tendency of their party to gain or lose. And we know that all are sure justice is on their side.

Probably it is impossible to dislodge party activists from positions that favour their parties but there is one particular point that even they really should consider. That is that the electoral system is very much a mechanism for taking *future* decisions. However much we work or argue, however much we debate and fight, and however public-spirited we may be, none of us can, today, decide who should win future elections. We cannot decide which as yet unknown or unborn party leaders will best serve their country in years to come. The only thing we might be able to do is design a system which will allow the voters of the future to reach collective decisions for the improvement of their society. If we feel any responsibility for the future, we will not design that system on the basis of our feelings for Miliband, Clegg and Cameron, because whatever their merits and demerits, they are snowflakes on the fire.

As a consequence of this outlook, this book may well be an uncomfortable one for politicians and for anyone firmly committed to one party or another. It should be, and I hope it is, because much of my argument is about defending democracy *against* politicians and the parties. Whatever unselfish and enlightened goals they may have, politicians' interests lie in gaining and holding power. This is an essential of their lives. They do not find every aspect of democracy convenient and, perhaps especially when it is inconvenient to them, it is important to us – the voters. It is the mechanism by which we control them. They do not want to be controlled but it is vital that they are.

I realise that my insistence on banishing the sentimentality of party loyalty and wishful thinking about the perfectibility of democracy might make my approach seem jaundiced, so let me be clear: I believe the system works extremely well. It *is* less than perfect but that is an earthly necessity and we dare not hope for perfection. There is simply no doubt that the forms of government reasonably described as 'democratic' have delivered far more good to their citizens and the world than any others.

The point of adopting this outlook is that the thing that makes our system work as well as it does is not the modesty of would-be leaders, the absence of clashes of interest or temper or the non-existence of naked ambition and simple greed. It is certainly not because if only we talk long enough, we will all agree. My argument is that the current voting system works as well as any is likely to, and it works well because it *harnesses* the dreams and aspirations of the power-hungry and the self-important, it constrains and controls political conflict and channels its energies towards the fulfilment of the public purpose. It comes as close as any system can to putting egotism at the service of the people.

1
THE NATURE OF DEMOCRACY

The extent to which democracy is simultaneously glorified and despised is remarkable. There is no end to the cynicism that many people feel about politicians, political parties or policies adopted just to win votes. Yet few would say they would rather the UK was *not* a democracy, and we fight wars not just to defend democracy but even to impose it. It is easy to see the source of both sentiments. Beside the hunger for power, the arrogance and the opportunism of our leaders lies the obvious fact that by and large, democracy has served civilisation a great deal better than any other form of government. Perhaps most pointedly, nothing has ever equalled it in allowing for a change of government without anyone having to die. So we should all be able to see what Winston Churchill had in mind with his not quite logical thought that democracy is the worst system except for all the others.

The explanation of why so many people have – some of the time – so much scepticism about democracy lies in a failure to think clearly about what democracy really does, or even what it can reasonably be expected to do, and about how it delivers its benefits. If we ask 'what is democracy?' there is a temptation to say 'rule by the people'. If we ask 'what are its benefits?' then the answer might be that it 'recognises and delivers political equality', that it 'puts power in the hands of voters', or something like that. The difficulty is that although these answers all sound wholesome, they take us nowhere in understanding the working of the system. And in any case, they are no more than aspirations. We need to be clear about those aspirations but we also need to see democracy's very severe limitations. More than this, we need to see specifically *how* it works to deliver the benefits and in what kind of circumstances – which we will wish to avoid – things might go seriously wrong.

Two questions lie at the heart of the issue. The first concerns the relationship between the voters and our elected representatives. When we vote for someone, what do we hope to achieve? To put it another way – what role can we realistically hope our elected representatives will perform?

The second is the issue of what role political parties and the party system have in a well-functioning democracy.

THREE VIEWS OF THE ELECTORAL PROCESS

There are, broadly speaking, three accounts of the role and nature of Parliament and MPs and hence of what the process of voting is trying to achieve. The first is that Parliament is first and foremost a place of deliberation; a place where things are argued about, minds are changed and, only then, decisions taken. On this view the role of voters is to select the candidate they feel has the soundest judgment and most open mind and the principal role of those elected as MPs is to exercise that judgment in the light of the debate they hear.

The second account is that the role of MPs is to represent electors' views and implement the policies they want. In this case, the role of voters is to select the candidate who adopts the policy programme nearest to their favoured one and the role of the elected would be to cast their votes to implement it.

The third account is that candidates are not so much pledged to policies as to support for certain people to form the government – especially for a particular person to be Prime Minister. Voters vote for the candidate who supports the individual they want to lead the government. The successful Prime Minister is then – at least in single-party government – more or less free to choose the rest of the government and the government is more or less free to implement its chosen policies, while being very substantially controlled by the Prime Minister.

There are, surely, elements of all three views in the minds of many voters and candidates. In both the operation of Parliament and of the electoral system one can see their traces. However, there are clear tensions between them. A candidate cannot both be committed to exercising independent judgment and to following a manifesto. Nor can a candidate be committed to a particular party, with a particular leader, on the basis that the party wishes that leader to be Prime Minister, and at the same time committed either to the exercise of independent judgment or the implementation of the party manifesto. There is no guarantee, after all, that leaders and their parties will implement their manifesto. So we should consider which, in the end, is the best description of what actually happens, as well as the question of how satisfactory a system it is.

In certain respects, we expect MPs to exercise independent judgment but, for the most part, we can rule out the idea that the House of Commons is a deliberative chamber. Perhaps in the eighteenth, or even the nineteenth century, there may have been reality in this view but today there is hardly any. There is practically no sign of members changing their minds because of debate – or not changing their votes, anyway. On the contrary, the government normally decides what legislation to propose and expects its supporters to vote for it. Deliberation and persuasion *within* the House of Commons are practically non-existent and certainly relate to no more than the details of proposals.

The second account has a much greater appearance of being a realistic description of how elections and Parliament work. Some elections have been – more or less – decided on the basis of clear positions on particular policies. The 1906 election, in which the issue of introducing a protectionist tariff was very prominent, is often given as an example. It is surely true that in 1983 Labour lost a large number of votes because of its promises to leave NATO and give up the UK's independent nuclear deterrent. It would be an exaggeration to say that either of these elections was determined by these issues but they clearly were important. The package of policies adopted by the Labour Party in 1945 – including the creation of the National Health Service and the great expansion of the welfare state – is perhaps another example but that was a very special case.

Parties do, of course, produce detailed manifestos and a good part of their argument is about future policy but this creates more of an illusion than a true picture. In a few cases, particular policy proposals might receive sufficient attention that they influence some voters, and these can become significant promises when a party is elected. They can also provide ammunition for the opposition when they are not implemented. But, taking the broad view, we have to be realistic both about how significant these things are and about how significant they could possibly be. For one thing, there is the simple and obvious point that most voters give very limited attention to most issues. Most people probably do not want to do more than that: for those who do not live and breathe politics, there are plenty of other things to do. Even if voters typically studied the details of the parties' stated platforms, the very fact that parties have a range of policies means that voters could, at most, only weigh up the package. Some people probably do that, although the question of how much time most people wish to spend doing it is important. Even if everybody did this, it would not mean we could have effective voter control of policy. If forty per cent of people vote for a certain party, the most that can be said is that those people preferred the package of policies it offered to any other package. If another twenty per cent vote for another party and these two parties happen to have a policy in common, we cannot say that sixty per cent of people support *that policy*. Where no other party advocated that policy, neither can we say that sixty per cent of people opposed it. If voters are taken as voting on the basis of policies, they can only be voting for packages. There is simply no other way.

Furthermore, a very large amount of policy – including some of the most important – is made between elections and arises from events which were not anticipated at the time of the election. Certainly people *might* vote on what parties promise about particular issues but those issues are not the only ones. None of the parties in the 1979 election said what they would do in the event of the Falkland Islands being invaded but when they were, the government had to decide. Gordon Brown and Alistair Darling said nothing during the 2005 election about how they would react to a financial crisis and the voters of May 2010 were offered no view on the question of whether Britain should contribute to the Irish banks bail-out. There are many, many much less newsworthy matters that governments must deal with but about which the voters are never consulted. Nor, realistically, could they be.

So, although the vision of voters choosing policy by electing MPs who share their view has its attractions, it is, in the end, thoroughly unrealistic. It is unrealistic both as a description of what does happen and as a description of what reasonably might happen. We have to accept that democracy cannot deliver that outcome, even if we would think it desirable for it to do so. If choosing policies is what democracy is meant to achieve, it is, most of the time, a very poor mechanism and – most importantly – that failing has nothing whatever to do with the voting system.

That leaves the third account: that the primary issue at stake in a general election is the selection of a Prime Minister and perhaps a small group of other ministers. In terms of explaining why elections are conducted in the way they are, this is a much better account than the others. Most notably, it explains why most voters seem quite content to cast a vote without knowing very much about the details of party policies: they are primarily choosing a leader, not a package of policies.

A particular illustration of this point comes from the televised debates during the 2010 election. There were three debates between the party leaders – the candidates to be Prime Minister – and one between the candidates to be Chancellor of the Exchequer. These were the choices really offered to the electorate – choices between the *people*. It would be interesting to know how many people (other than party activists) can remember what answers were given to policy questions but the outcome, particularly of the first party leaders' debate, is memorable: 'Election debate: Nick Clegg emerges victorious' according to the *Daily Telegraph*,[1] 'Nick Clegg now in contention as potential PM' (the *Guardian*[2]) and 'Nick Clegg seizes his moment in historic TV debate' (*The Times*[3]). Every time, the person won. Where were the headlines saying 'Voters persuaded by Lib Dem policy proposals'?

Another point that arises from these debates is the issue of what the reaction would have been if one of the leaders had sent someone else in his place, with full authority to state policy. If we were choosing the policies, it should not matter, but the point was that what was wanted was a debate between the people who were offering themselves as our leader. Anyone sending a deputy would have been ridiculed and destroyed.

A watered-down version of the view that voters choose policies is sometimes suggested as a serviceable idea. The suggestion is that the parties have an identifiable general approach and voters select the approach they like best. However, detailed analysis makes it rather hard to give proper substance to this idea. It would be a common claim, for example, that Conservatives are in favour of 'small government' but the Thatcher government showed few signs. The Blair government was elected with a commitment to the general principles of civil liberties and the importance of the individual. Through a variety of measures – notably the Freedom of Information Act – they clearly worked in that direction but they also gave us Control Orders. Liberal Democrats persistently tell us that they believe in individual freedom, so we might have expected them to vote (for example) against smoking bans. When it came to it, they had reasons for voting for them. We might agree that they were very good reasons but they were not reasons that emphasised the rights of individual freedom.

Another point is that some of the things said about these 'general approaches' are really just attacks by supporters of one party on another. If we hear it said that Conservatives tend to protect the interests of the privileged or that Labour favours top-down management, it is pretty certain that the claims are being made by their opponents. However, what parties say about themselves – such as that they are in favour of maximising the benefits of individual initiative or creating a fairer society – are things that no one would be likely to find objectionable. Who believes in suppressing initiative or creating an unfair society? The lesson is that general approaches are either aspects of the rhetorical posturing which is an inevitable part of political argument or they are more or less infinitely elastic, so that they offer next to no guidance as to what a party might actually do. If we want to know what parties intend to do if they are elected (or what they want us to believe they will do), we have to find out about their policy commitments. But that is precisely what most of us do not much want to be bothered with.

It is no failing in the voters to treat the identity of the party leaders as more important than the policy. The details of policy are complicated and, for the most part, boring. Occasionally, policy debate might feature prominently and then voters can and do take note of what is being offered. But even when that is true – which is only sometimes – it is only true of a very small number of policies, not the whole range. The rest of the time, we are simply in the position of recognising that policy issues need to be handled well but that our best shot at achieving this is to select a person who will select a team to do it, not to try to fathom them ourselves. Since we cannot possibly know what issues will arise after an election, it is important that we select people we believe will handle them well.

In this vision, which was most famously expounded by Joseph Schumpeter in his great work *Capitalism, Socialism and Democracy,*[4] elections are about the selection of leaders. The policies they propose at election time, and their effectiveness in arguing for them, no doubt contribute to voters' decisions but the policies themselves are not the primary concern. Schumpeter was not especially concerned with proportional representation but he did note that this draws the sting from the argument for it. If we are voting for policies, the idea that in the absence of a majority there is an important role for compromise clearly has some appeal. However, we cannot have a proportionally representative Prime Minister. We cannot have forty per cent Cameron, thirty-five per cent Brown, twenty-three per cent Clegg and the little left over shared among the others. We can only have one. So this view starts to call into question the desirability of proportional representation. Sir Karl Popper emphasised a further point: *selecting* leaders very often really means *dismissing* those we have.[5] Elections are, as he later put it, the 'Day of Judgment' for those in power; the opportunity for the voters to remove their leaders. In this view, of course, there is no issue at all about proportionality. Either the Prime Minister must stay or the Prime Minister must go.

As a description of what actually occurs, this view has a great deal going for it. Not many people know much about the parties' manifestos but they do assess the parties' leaders, sometimes very critically. As a description of what reasonably *might* occur, this account is also well ahead of its rivals. We *can* assess the leaders and, up to a point, their teams. This is very much easier than assessing policy at anything approaching the level of detail that would be required to form a judgment of which party to support. Similarly, whereas we cannot decide in advance what policy should be followed in unknown circumstances, we can judge those who might have to make it and, even more clearly, we can judge those who have been making it for us. It would be entirely futile to expect Gordon Brown to have told us in 2005 what he would do in the event of the financial crisis but in 2010 we certainly could make an assessment of what he actually did. If democracy is seen as a system that permits the governed to select those who govern and elections as the process by which they are selected and dismissed, it can be seen as being very effective.

On this basis, it could be questioned whether we really need to bother with most of what happens in Parliament. It seems as if the Prime Minister ought to be regarded more as a president[6] and if that is the way it is, we could just as well directly elect the President. A case could certainly be made that it would be a good idea to undertake such a major constitutional change but this issue really plays no part in the debate over voting reform, since it is not on the agenda. It certainly has to be admitted, though, that much of what goes on in Parliament is thoroughly inconsequential. It has its rituals: the Queen's Speech, the Opening of Parliament and all that. There are incidental opportunities for individual politicians to advance their careers, for example by saying things they hope will be reported – to their advantage – in their local newspapers. There are occasional opportunities for the House of Commons to operate as a deliberative chamber, in which opinions can actually be changed. Slightly more often, there is the opportunity for a free vote, in which the parties permit members to vote according to their personal views. The promise of such a vote on foxhunting shows that this does happen, although the fact that this issue even comes to attention hardly suggests that the House of Commons is much of a real debating chamber.

More importantly, however, parliamentary debate serves one clear function, which is that the arguments and responses expressed in the House of Commons are, very definitely, on the record. When the Government says it does something for a certain reason and the Opposition says it ought not to because certain adverse consequences will result, these exchanges are preserved. Some of the ammunition of future electoral battle is manufactured here and it provides a basis on which both Government and Opposition can be judged. In this way, the spectacle of parliamentary contest, artificial though some aspects are, feeds the democratic process.

It should be noted, too, that this is not only a good description of what happens, but a description of a very good system. The 'Day of Judgment' is no mere theatrical image – it is a rather precise description. Our leaders stand to lose all their power when we say so. And the threat of that retrospective judgment is ever-present during the life of a government. It is a certainty of political life in an effective democracy that the day will come when the voters exercise their judgment and no politician ever forgets it.

Since the Day of Judgment is always in the politician's mind, it always affects political activity. There will be cases where particular promises have been prominent enough in policy debate for it to be important that they are kept. There will also be the opportunity for taking hard decisions early in a Parliament, in the hope of a return by its end. The budget cuts of 2010, whether they are good or bad policy, obviously fall into this category. Failing this, there is the opportunity for the exercise of leadership in persuading the voters that these were the right things to do, even if they have unpleasant consequences. Or there is the possibility of persuading the voters that the people who took those decisions should be trusted to take more. No doubt, as elections draw closer, the temptation to give the voters what they want, rather than to seek to persuade them of the benefits of anything else, will always grow. That is more or less inevitable in a democracy. The more important point is that the fine balance our leaders try to strike is the one that will see them re-elected. The significance of the ambition to be re-elected is great. It is surely a far more powerful force in keeping our leaders seeking to govern well than is any slight control voters might have over specific policy promises.

So, the view that our leaders are selected by us, expected to do their best and then be assessed on their record is not a pessimistic view of the potential of democracy. Rather, it says that so long as our leaders are power-hungry, arrogant and opportunistic, power lies where it belongs: with the voters. We cannot separately assess each and every policy of the government but we can decide whether the leaders we have should continue or whether they should go. When we decide that they should go, democracy furnishes the tools with which we can make it happen. Perhaps even more importantly, the threat of rejection keeps the government working to avoid that outcome. Even if it is only a coincidence, it is highly important that, of the three views of democracy, only one is a realistic description of what happens and that is the only one that makes democracy seem effective. The power of the people to dismiss the government is the greatest gift of democracy and should be treasured.

THE PARTY SYSTEM

The three views of the function of Parliament give rise to different attitudes to the party system and the proper role of political parties. Whether we believe that Parliament is a place of deliberation or that we elect members because of their specific policy pledges, it is just about possible to imagine a Parliament without parties. In that case voters vote for the people or the policies they favoured and the MPs would vote accordingly.

In reality, MPs are normally expected to vote according to their party's wishes and to the (usually considerable) extent that they do, they cannot be said to be exercising useful independent judgment. Whatever policy views they may have, they suppress. This is probably inevitable. The inducements for members to form themselves into parties are simply too strong. Imagine two members who agree on most issues but disagree on others. Of their disagreements, they regard some as important and some as unimportant. The temptation to bargain away a vote on an 'unimportant' issue in exchange for one on an 'important' issue is obvious and powerful. How could it be any other way? There is the beginning of a party.

On the first view, the formation of parties could be seen as a serious failing. Members are specifically elected to exercise independent judgment and the creation of parties means they are not doing so. The stronger the party discipline that develops, the greater the problem. Circumstances like recent ones, in which for the most part party discipline is pretty strong, are a reason to reject deliberation as a reasonable description of Parliament. But the inevitability of party formation warns against the Utopianism that longs for a Parliament without parties.

On the second view, the matter is not quite so serious. If there must be parties, at least voters can vote for the party with the collection of policies nearest to what they would like. There is no basic dishonesty about it. However, the fact that most candidates are signed up to a collection of policies limits the voters' choice. Where party discipline prevents elected members from deviating from the party position, it is a principal factor in condemning the voters' choice of policy to ineffectiveness. The voters can only ever choose from the party positions and these are never going to offer many options. If we start with this view of what democracy and elections are about, a loosening of party discipline could seem very desirable. Some say proportional representation, particularly versions that allow voters to select between candidates of the same party, offers this possibility. However, it requires voters to take note of the details not only of parties' but of candidates' policies and for those elected to be free from party discipline. Even that gives voters only as many options as there are candidates: nowhere near enough for the range of policies on offer.[7] This road again leads to pessimism about the potentials of democracy.

On the third view – that we are really selecting leaders, not policies – the existence of parties is not only inevitable but, in a parliamentary democracy, practically essential. If voters are to express preferences over who should be Prime Minister, it is essential that the candidates are tied to particular individuals who are the candidates for that job. Party discipline is the means by which they are tied. If the voters elect a leader on the basis that the leader will – broadly speaking – be the one to lead policy making, it is important that the leader is able to make policy. That means that there must be a more-or-less reliable body of MPs who will, to put it simply, do as they are told. Consequently, although political parties are often thought of as nothing more than parasites, it would be better to see them as useful bacteria, cleansing the body politic of indecision, muddle and confusion. Without a reasonably firm party system, it is the voters who lose.

CONSTITUTIONAL REFORM AND THE VOTING SYSTEM

The argument is nowhere near complete but some conclusions can be drawn. One concerns the paradox with which I began this chapter. Those who believe that democracy should be the means by which the voters select policy are doomed to be disappointed. It can hardly do that at all. Those who believe they are selecting wise people to deliberate among themselves will certainly be no happier. They are selecting amongst party troops, who, as far as voting for legislation is concerned, almost always follow orders. Yet, seen another way, the value of democracy comes to life. So long as our leaders remain hungry for power, as they surely will, we can rely on the Day of Judgment to keep their minds on the job of serving our interests.

With this view in mind it is possible to start to see responses to the case for proportional representation. Three of the subsidiary arguments deserve attention: that the current system generates large changes in party representation in Parliament from much smaller changes in voting patterns, that reform would weaken the power of the parties and the claim that it would make politics less confrontational and more co-operative.

The generation of large swings in seats is one of the characteristics of the British system that gives power to the Day of Judgment. It gives voters the strength properly to discipline a government. In a proportional system the loss of a few votes would, obviously, lead to a loss of seats in about the same proportion, so we might expect that the government (probably a coalition government, under proportional representation) would very often stay the same.

There is rough justice in a system that creates large swings in seats but it is rough justice only for the politicians. They might not like it but that is not the point. The voters' power flows from it and the forces of political self-interest are encouraged by it. It is a very naïve view that counts this as a limitation of the system.

Even with this system, to be able to make use of their power, voters need a party structure. Whether proportional representation would weaken the party system is a question to which I shall return but even if it does, it is hard to see how it would help voters take reasoned decisions about whether to support the government or reject it. Without a reasonably clear party system, every situation would appear to the voters as a shambles, an incalculable mass of competing voices. They would be unable to exercise any reasonable judgment and for practical purposes would have nothing to go on in deciding how to vote. For the most part, it is the party system that makes it possible for voters to exercise informed judgment. The Day of Judgment exists but to have its full power, we must be quite clear who are supporters of the government and who are not. So we need the party system.

As to making the system less confrontational, this too is misunderstood by advocates of proportional representation. Confrontation may be the most essential of all the ingredients of democracy. There can only be one government at a time; for a workable democracy, it must be vulnerable to the electorate. For that reason, there must also be an alternative government in waiting. The alternative government must make the best case it can for replacing the existing one, and the voters should want it to. It does not help voters exercise their judgment if the Opposition is spending its energies on cultivating good manners and herbaceous borders. We should want them to go out of their way to find the weaknesses of the Government's position and explain them to the electorate. We are then empowered to make a choice. Indeed, it is practically essential that the Opposition should be so engaged, because there is far too much information for ordinary citizens to make much headway. I suggested earlier that parliamentary debate serves the function of putting positions on the record. It does; but most of those positions are pretty uninteresting. If the Government makes a mistake, we the voters, most of the time, need someone to tell us about it. Fortunately, the system gives the Opposition every incentive to do just that. Although some of these attacks seem puerile and we can despair of the quality of political debate, there is a much more optimistic view: when it becomes apparent that the Opposition's attacks on the Government are entirely trivial or meritless, the voters learn a great deal. We learn they have nothing better to say. So we can presume the Government is doing well. We need the puerile efforts of the Opposition if we are to learn this, since we are not likely to be convinced of it just because the Government says so. Adversarialism has, therefore, an *essential* role in effective democracy.

This point is crucially important but taking the argument as it is made by the reformists, it arises only from a subsidiary point of their case. Nevertheless, we can perhaps see the greater case for proportional representation being weakened. Once politics is seen as a contest between the government and those who would replace it, the existence of multiple possible replacements is clearly just a distraction and the significance of their separate identities pales. The position is that we have a government and the big choice confronting us at an election is simply whether we want it to continue. If not, we must hope that there is an opposition ready and willing to take over.

This is only the beginning of the argument. The case against reform has started to be made but there is one point – one glaring point – which has not been mentioned. It is a point that features in every argument for proportional representation; indeed it is often the only point. It was the principal argument of the Jenkins Report and nearly everyone else among the reformists. Quite simply, it is that the current system is unfair, and whatever else it is, a democracy must be fair.

2
WHAT ARE 'FAIR VOTES'?

The idea that proportional representation is 'fair' is, time and again, placed at the centre of its advocates' case. They recite a string of statistics showing, in numerous different ways, that the current system often results in parliaments in which the proportion of seats is different from the proportion of votes. Applied to the 2010 election, they might tell us that the Liberal Democrats had twenty-three per cent of the vote and the Conservatives thirty-six per cent but that this brought the Liberal Democrats nine per cent of the seats and the Conservatives forty-seven per cent. The same fact might then be repeated in the form that there is one Liberal Democrat MP for every 120,000 votes but one Conservative for every 35,000. They might then go on to say that in the South East, Labour had sixteen per cent of the vote and about five per cent of the seats, whereas in London their thirty-seven per cent of the vote won fifty-two per cent of the seats.[1] This will then be rounded off with a demand for 'fair votes' and that is taken to make the whole case.

One response – often used by the opponents of proportional representation – is to say that proportional systems lead to weak and ineffective government. That amounts to saying that we have to decide between fairness and good government. Surely anyone will admit that if that is the choice, it might be a difficult one, but it will have to be made. Indeed it would but there is plenty more to be considered before we get to that point.

The first step is to challenge the idea of 'fairness' and to show how very seriously limited it is in precisely those areas where it is so important to the case for proportional representation. Fairness is not unimportant – certainly not – but it is a much more complex idea than reformists acknowledge. There are no simple formulae that tell us one thing is fair and another is not; there is just a collection of difficult questions. Once we see this, I believe, the force of this particular part of the case for electoral reform is enormously weakened. It seems at first to be overwhelmingly powerful but in fact gives very little, if any, strength to the case for reform.

We should begin by asking to whom we are trying to be 'fair'; then ask what we mean by 'fairness' and finally see what the possibilities are. That is, we have to see how much 'fairness', and of what kind, it is possible for a voting system to deliver. We also have to consider where the attempt to create 'fairness' – in whatever sense that is possible – leads and whether the consequences themselves would be fair or desirable. In the end, I believe that the *most* we can hope for from an electoral system is not very much. The danger is that a great deal could be given up trying to get it.

FAIRNESS TO WHOM?

The first question is whether we are trying to be fair to politicians, to parties or to voters. There are certainly ways in which we would want to be fair to all of them. It is important that electoral rules are followed, that the votes are correctly counted and so on. But on the question of the fairness of the voting system, the claims of parties and politicians should be quickly dismissed. Politicians are people who offer themselves in the hope of winning great power and prestige. They have their chance, in elections, to make their case to the voters and they are either elected or they are not. If they do not like the result, it is just their bad luck. Those who go into politics accept the luck of the draw in these matters and take the rough with the smooth. The verdict of the electors is final. Similarly, political parties are essential to the effective operation of advanced democracy but they are also basically organisations through which politicians contest with each other for power. They are, as I have said, much like parasites. If some of the parasites do not get their fair go at government that too is bad luck.

The idea that we should design a system that is fair to voters has much more appeal. Indeed, this is precisely the view initially taken by the Jenkins Commission: 'Fairness to voters is the first essential … Parties should, like the electoral system, be servants rather than masters'. As they also said, quite rightly, the *manifestation* of unfairness to voters might be measured by the results for the parties but that does not change the fact that what we want to avoid is unfairness to the voters. It is easy enough to see where this argument leads. Indeed, the second form of the usual presentation of statistics is aimed directly at it. If there is one Liberal Democrat MP for every 120,000 Liberal Democrat voters but one Conservative MP for every 35,000 voters, is it not clear that this is unfair to the Liberal Democrat *voters*?

There is certainly common sense in that view and it is probably the essence of the point made by advocates of proportional representation which has most practical weight in arguments about the issue. But common sense is not always right.

WHAT IS FAIRNESS?

There are many kinds of fairness and it is important to be clear both what kind we are discussing and why that particular kind of fairness is important to the person or organisation in question in the context of an election.

The issue of why fairness is important might seem a strange one; it might seem fairness is always important. But consider some examples. The Olympic high jump competition tends to be won by tall people. Is it an unfair competition because short people are disadvantaged? In a way it is, but not in the way that is taken to be relevant to the competition in question. We could imagine a system of different gold medals for people of different heights, which would produce results which were fair in a different way. Golf has a handicapping system which is used in some competitions. Such systems could be devised for other sports. So, for example, with a little ingenuity and quite a lot of statistical analysis, it is possible to devise a formula to say whether a fifty-two-year old man could be said to have fairly beaten a twenty-eight-year old woman in the Great North Run – it might be more than just a matter of their times.[2] It should be clear that different contexts demand different ideas of what makes for a fair competition. There is no single, unique, idea of 'fairness'.

Moving back to the matter of electoral rules, here is a possibility: one way of selecting an MP would be to invite residents of the constituency to say whether they would be willing to serve, and then to select the Member from the willing by lottery. Everyone who wanted to be an MP would then have an equal chance of being selected. There is an obvious sense in which this would be fair but it would not be sensible, because it would, no doubt, result in the selection of many unsuitable people. But that is another matter. Some might also think that it would not be democratic, since it would not reflect the preferences of the voters. However, Classical Athens filled some official posts by lottery and it forms the basis of jury selection today; and neither of those is usually treated as a great example of something seriously undemocratic. The fact that there is a *kind* of fairness in the lottery system is a useful reminder that no form of democratic selection has a unique claim to being 'fair selection'.

There are other difficulties of the same general family. One thing that cannot be delivered by any of the proportional representation systems normally suggested is any sense of the strength of individual voters' views. Again, to see the point, we must think about it specifically and only as a point about fairness. What makes it *fair* that the views of someone with a strong preference should have the same weight as those of someone who does not much mind who wins but turns up to vote out of civic duty? There would certainly be difficulties in assessing strength of feeling if we wanted to but that is not a point about fairness. The real answer is that the system is a one-voter, one-vote system and we have the view that this is fair. But that is a decision or an attitude we have, not a fact about 'fairness'.

We could also consider the case of voters who take much more care than others in considering their decision. One diligently reads all the manifestos, attends meetings to hear the candidates, asks pertinent questions, takes careful notes, then retires for a couple of days of quiet contemplation to decide who to support. The other reaches the polling booth without a thought about it and then votes for the candidate whose name has the most vowels.[3] Why is it *fair* that their votes count the same? The answer is simple enough: there is no unique basis of 'fairness' which makes it so. It is just the way we decide to have it done.

WHAT CAN VOTING ACHIEVE?

A natural response to these kinds of question is perhaps to say that a fair voting system is the one that best translates the voters' preferences into political decisions embodying society's preference. There are some difficulties about what we mean by 'voters' preferences' (which will be considered in the next section) but rather more fundamentally, there are problems about what sort of 'translation' might even be possible.

The major, fundamental, difficulty is that the preferences of individuals can be such that there is no reasonable basis on which we can say what the 'preference of the community' is. The nature of the problem is easily demonstrated by a very simple example.

Consider three voters, A, B and C, who have three choices as to how to vote: square, triangle and circle. (It does not matter whether the 'choices' are thought of as candidates, parties, alternative policies, or alterative manifestos.) A prefers square, with triangle second and circle third; B prefers triangle, with circle second and square third; C prefers circle, with square second and triangle third. So, the voters' rankings are these:

A: square – triangle – circle
B: triangle – circle – square
C: circle – square – triangle

Which should win? In a vote between square and triangle, A and C vote for square, so it wins. In a vote between circle and square, B and C vote for circle, so it wins. That seems to tell us that circle is better than square and square is better than triangle, so it seems obvious that circle must be better than triangle too. But no, because in a vote between these two, A and B vote for triangle. So does that mean that triangle is better than circle, circle is better than square *and* square is better than triangle? If we met an individual with preferences like that we would surely think a mistake had been made somewhere. But as this example shows, when we are dealing with a group of individuals, different rules apply.

It is true that a particular way of voting will result in a particular outcome. If, for example, there is a vote between square and triangle, followed by a vote between the winner and circle, the outcome is that square wins on the first round and circle becomes the final winner on the second. However, if the procedure is that the first vote is between triangle and circle, then triangle wins, square wins on the second round and we reach a different result. Clearly, there is no basis for saying that one order of voting is better than another. What this example lacks is anything that could reasonably be called the 'right' or 'fair' answer. Particular systems give particular results but none has a better claim than others to being the correct result.

We might say that any one of the decisions is as good as any other, so that neither issues of fairness nor effectiveness arise. But this is only the simplest version of the problem and it is easy enough to find cases that would be more problematic. Consider this case, where there is a nasty problem:

Group 1 consists of 100 people who rank the options
    square – triangle – circle
Group 2 consists of 150 who rank them triangle – circle
    – square

Group 3 consists of 200 who rank them circle – square – triangle

Here, circle is the most popular in terms of first preferences (having 200) and the most popular in terms of first and second preferences added together (having 350). Looking at all the numbers like this, common sense surely says circle should win. However, notice this. If the voting system happens to demand that the first vote is between triangle and circle and the second between the winner of that competition and square, circle loses on the first round, because groups 1 and 2 both prefer triangle to circle. (For the purpose of describing the problem, I am ignoring the possibility of tactical voting.) So the idea from the first example that it would not much matter which voting procedure is followed is clearly not generally true. In the first case, in which one person favoured each option, there was no way to say what outcome was 'fair'. In the second case, the clear common sense result and one possible election result are different.

Here is a variation which is even more worrying. Suppose we add the oblong party, so there are four options, and the three voters rank them best to worst like this:

Voter A ranks them: oblong – square – triangle – circle
Voter B ranks them: circle – oblong – square – triangle
Voter C ranks them: triangle – circle – oblong – square

Again, suppose that the election runs on the basis of a head-to-head between two options, with the winner then going head-to-head with one of the others and the winner of that contesting with the last one for the final decision. If the first vote is between circle and oblong, both B and C vote for circle, so it wins. If the next is between circle and triangle, A and C vote for triangle which therefore wins and if the third is between triangle and square, A and B will vote for square, making it the final winner. That is all well and good until we notice that oblong is preferred to square by *all* the voters. Which one is the 'right' answer, the 'fair' answer or the democratic answer? And these problems are only illustrative of the general nature of the issue. There are many 'voting paradoxes' along these lines.[4] The lesson of these examples is that there can be no general argument as to what is a fair system – depending on how we look at particular problems, different things seem fair. In trying to devise a system to handle them all, we are very poorly placed.

Some people might feel these sorts of problems are not very likely to occur. There are two responses to that: one is to say that it is not really relevant, since the point is to explore the idea of 'fairness'. These sorts of examples show that there can be no straightforward and general idea of 'fairer' or 'more democratic' in cases where there is more to voting than simply selecting between two options. So whatever it is people want when they want 'fairness' is going to be much harder to define than it seems. There are *no* simple answers.

The second response is to ask what makes it seem unlikely that any of these problems will emerge? Indeed, if voter preferences are simply for party labels or party leaders and if the general tendency is for Labour and Conservative supporters both to prefer the Liberal Democrats to the other major party then it is unlikely that such cycles will emerge. To put it very simply, if a sufficiently high proportion of people rank one of the parties – the Liberal Democrats, presumably – either first or second, these sorts of problems cannot arise. (A similar rule applies to four-party systems.) However, if voters' preferences are really based on the selection of policies it is much more likely that they will emerge. In this case, any of the party manifestos might offer them what they want on the issues they regard as important, and any of the others might be their second choice. Even if it were true that the Liberal Democrats tended to take a middling position between the other parties on each issue (which, probably, it is not), the fact that there is a collection of different issues, each of a different degree of importance in the view of each voter, would mean that there would be no predictability about second choices.

We might draw from this the lesson that the feeling that 'voting cycles' like those described above are unlikely is itself evidence that most people really feel that they are voting for the individuals who are the leaders of a party and that the issue of policy selection is, as I suggested in Chapter 1, not nearly as important as is often suggested. In any case, the wider lesson of these sorts of issues is that the idea that the best voting system is the one that gives the best measure of the community's preference faces a very serious difficulty. That cannot be the *key* to designing a voting system, because the thing supposedly being identified – the community's preference – might not even really exist.

WHAT DO WE KNOW ABOUT VOTERS' PREFERENCES?

Such voting cycles are not inevitable; some will think they are not likely but in any case, we will have to live with it. We should be warned that there are logical limits to what voting systems can ever achieve. Despite the problems, we have to carry on thinking about the issue: first, because we still need a voting system, and second, because such problems are only the beginning.

The arguments that move rapidly from numbers of votes for each party to conclusions about what would constitute a 'fair' number of MPs for that party make a number of very dubious presumptions. Some are occasionally recognised: for example, the fact that people vote for a member who works hard in the constituency should not really be taken as indicating anything at all about the party composition of Parliament. If Liberal Democrat MPs tend to be hard workers for their constituents and gain votes for that, adding up those votes tells us nothing about how those voters feel about the overall composition of the House of Commons. That is obvious and beyond dispute but it might reasonably be said that the numbers involved are small and the problem is not too serious. There is also the recognised issue of tactical voting, when voters choose to vote for a party they do not support to try to defeat one they regard as worse. That alone calls into question the translation from votes to seats used by the advocates of proportional representation.

There are other problems of this general character. There might be protest votes: votes cast for candidates who are confidently expected to lose, for the purpose of registering dissatisfaction with the other choices on offer. There might also be people who vote for *some* representation of a particular party, without any sort of desire that it should form the government. In the 2010 election, for example, Caroline Lucas, of the Green Party, was elected MP for the Brighton Pavilion constituency. It was known during the campaign that there was a significant Green challenge in that seat (and only in that seat, realistically). It seems almost certain that some of those who voted for her did so because they thought it would be desirable for there to be a Green

Party MP. In that case we can conclude nothing about the 'fair' number of Green Party MPs from adding up the votes for that party. A related point arises in relation to hung parliaments. In the last days of the 2010 election campaign, when a hung parliament seemed very likely, the Conservative Party used a Party Election Broadcast to say that (as they thought) such an outcome would in itself be damaging. We may presume they thought this would be effective in swaying voters away from the Liberal Democrats. Indeed, the opinion polls recorded a fall in support for that party. After the election, even Lord Paddy Ashdown – a former leader of the Liberal Democrats – seemed to think that the likelihood of a hung parliament had changed voting intentions, saying that 'fear' had driven voters away from the Liberal Democrats.[5] The voters concerned were therefore not voting for the *party* they wanted to win. They were, presumably, voting for *someone* to win. Another possibility is that some of those who voted Liberal Democrat would specifically have preferred a hung parliament to one-party government. In voting, they would have been hoping for a good-sized body of Liberal Democrat MPs, able to exert significant influence over the government, presumably in coalition. It does not follow that they would have wished for a Liberal Democrat government. Their first choice of *single-party* government might be any party. They need not even have had a particular preference about just how many

WHAT ARE 'FAIR VOTES'?

Liberal Democrat MPs there were to be. Their hope may have been no more specific than that there would be enough to have some influence. On what basis could anyone say that the actual outcome was unfair to those voters? They have just what they wanted.

The point is not whether hung parliaments are or are not desirable. Rather, it is that one of the considerations voters might have in mind when casting their vote is the question of what kind of overall composition of the House of Commons they are hoping to achieve. Once we admit possibilities like these, we can neither make inferences from the number of votes cast for a party to the number of voters who want it to form a government, nor to what proportion of the Parliament any voter would think it desirable for that party to hold. Some of the voters are simply not expressing that kind of view; they are using their vote intelligently to try to bring about the kind of overall result they regard as desirable.

There is also an issue about what gives special weight to the currently existing parties. What do we say about 'fairness' to voters who would like to vote for a party which happens not to be standing, or indeed, may not even exist? It is perhaps natural enough that the politicians, who are more or less all party-people, do not often see the importance of this, but if what we want is a Parliament that 'fairly reflects voters' views', we are out of luck. It is a fact of life that voters choose between the candidates who are standing. The 'fairness' of the reflection of their views over such a narrow choice can only ever be a very limited kind of fairness.

This point consistently escapes the reformists. For example, Enid Lakeman – a long-term campaigner for proportional representation and sometime Director of the Electoral Reform Society – could not have been more precisely wrong when she said that, under the Single Transferable Vote (a voting system with several members for each constituency), 'five or so' members per constituency would make for 'reasonably fair representation'.[6] That may be about right when there are only three parties worthy of consideration but what if there are six or more? Significant (but less popular) parties would still not be represented. Her conviction that the current list of parties has some special status in arguments about fairness led to her conclusion, but while it is *fairness* that we are thinking about, the view that the current parties are the only ones that matter has nothing at all going for it.

The consequence is that even on the issue that seems to give the advocates of proportional representation their strongest point the extent of that point is very limited. We could make the proportion of seats of each party conform to the proportion of votes but that is about the most that can be done. If we are interested in fairness, that is not much.

Even on the question of fairness, though, this is only a preliminary. A very significant further problem remains.

'FAIRNESS' IN THE COMPOSITION OF A GOVERNMENT

An aspect of the question of electoral reform which is hardly ever given more than the most superficial consideration is that of whether the formation of coalition governments ought to be regarded as fair to voters. I shall consider wider questions about coalition – which are substantial – in Chapter 3 but here, the issue is that of fairness to voters. For the moment, I shall temporarily assume that there are no serious issues about the stability, effectiveness or legitimacy of coalition.

In so far as the reformists consider this question, all they seem to say is that a proportional representation system would probably result in coalition government and if it did, a virtue of the system would be that the government would have the support of a majority of voters. That, I suppose, could be treated as a claim that it is fair to voters. However, it is a remarkable claim and it is remarkable too how little it is challenged, since it is quite plainly false.

No one voted for the current coalition. No such grouping was on the ballot paper. (Some people might have been hoping for such a coalition but that is another matter;

they actually voted for one of the parties.) Nor did anyone vote for the policy programme implemented by the coalition. To put the matter bluntly, the doctrine that coalitions have majority support amounts to saying that all those who voted Liberal Democrat when they were promised no increases in university tuition fees are to be counted as part of a majority which now supports the raising of such fees. Those who voted Conservative and who did not want a referendum on the alternative vote are – I suppose – to be counted in a majority who did. That is clearly a nonsense.

One view might be that parties which agree to this kind of thing should be condemned for it but, as a general proposition, that is unrealistic. Coalition *must* involve some kind of compromise. It is just that although a compromise policy may have all kinds of things to be said for it, the claim that it has the majority support of the voters can hardly be one of them. A similar – and true – point is that the coalition is composed of individual MPs who represent parties for which a majority of voters voted. However, the difference between this and the claim that the coalition itself has won the majority support of the electorate is highly significant. For one thing, again, we see that the real argument must be one about the leaders, *not* their policies. The general feeling that it is somehow fair to the voters that Liberal Democrat and Conservative leaders settle policy between themselves

– precisely what they have done – must come from the feeling that voters elect the leaders much more than they select the policies. The leaders then do what they want.

Another aspect of the problem that is sometimes raised is whether, in proportional systems, the parties end up with a fair share of positions in government over a period of time. Various studies of this have been undertaken but Michael Pinto-Duschinsky – a rare academic opponent of proportional representation – has made an interesting claim about (West) Germany.[7] He said that between 1949 and 1998, the Free Democrats had averaged nine per cent of the vote but had (through coalition) been in government for eighty-six per cent of the time and that across the whole period had held nineteen per cent of the posts in the Cabinet. The Social Democrats, meanwhile, had averaged thirty-seven per cent of the vote but been in power only twenty-one per cent of the time and held, on average, twenty-one per cent of the posts in the Cabinet. These figures are explained by the fact that the Free Democrats, being a small centrist party, in what was more or less a three-party system, were able to extract a high price for their support. The fact that the proportion of seats they had was more or less the same as the proportion of the votes they won clearly does not exhaust the issue of fairness. Why is it fair that this little party had on average about as many people in the Cabinet as a party scoring around four times as many votes?

THE CASE AGAINST VOTING REFORM

There is another way of looking at the issue of the fairness of the composition of governments. As Pinto-Duschinsky treated it, the issue was about the share in government over a long period of time but what about the share of government in each Parliament? In exactly the same way in which the reformists say that twenty-nine per cent of people voted Labour, so that 'fair votes' would mean that 189 MPs should be Labour, rather than the 258 actually elected, how can it be fair that *none* of the Cabinet is Labour? Even if we accept that in the circumstances in which proportional representation has been implemented a parliamentary majority has the backing of a majority of voters – dubious as that claim is – it takes us nowhere. The dispute is not about whether a parliamentary majority can form a government. It is about why it is fair to the people who voted for other parties to have no part in that government. Given the reformists' attitude to 'fairness to voters', this should be a crucial point: instead, it is ignored. What principle says that if a party has twenty-nine per cent of the votes, fairness demands that it must have twenty-nine per cent of the MPs but does not go on to say that it must have twenty-nine per cent of the posts in the government as well?

It is just possible that someone might try to escape from this problem by claiming that Parliament is the true legislative body and the Cabinet is subservient to it, so that representation in Parliament is the crucial thing. But as far as the actual operation of the system is concerned, there is no merit in that view. Most of the time, the government decides policy and relies on its parliamentary majority to implement it. If there is a limit on what it can do because of what the backbenchers will or will not accept – and there is evidence that this happens[8] – the crucial people are the backbenchers of the governing party (or coalition). That says nothing about the non-governing parties having a practical share in policy-making, so we must look elsewhere for an explanation of why this point gets no attention.

The reformists do not reach the conclusion their argument demands, because they recognise that the idea of proportional representation in the government is a recipe for disaster; it would amount to the abolition of parliamentary opposition. Everyone would be on the side of the government and the voters would have no true choices at all. I have already argued that a good dose of adversarialism is essential to effective democracy but the idea that all parties should share in government goes well beyond diminishing adversarialism. The spectacle of Prime Minister's Question Time may sometimes be unedifying but imagine a version in which the only questions came from the Prime Minister's supporters and nothing was asked other than to invite the PM to agree that the government was pursuing the best of all possible policies. In such a situation, a government could be changed only by the election of one which previously had no parliamentary position at all, since only such groups would be part of the 'opposition'. It would be a catastrophe for democracy.

Each party would be safe to share out the spoils. There would be no Day of Judgment and this would certainly be the victory of the Parties over the People. The fact that the reformists do not contemplate such a thing also shows that they do not really, or at least not consistently, accord such a central role to 'fairness'.

Conclusion

We now see further cracks in the case for proportional representation. The central claim of the whole position – its claim to 'fairness' – is much more difficult than it is ever allowed to seem by its advocates. It is not that fairness is unimportant; it is that before we even start we have to admit that it is problematic and there are no clear answers as to what is fair. Then there is the problem of taking individual choices and amalgamating them into something we might call 'society's choice'. This presents logical difficulties to which there can be no solution. We simply cannot tell enough about voters' preferences – they might be voting for all kinds of things other than a choice of government. And when we recognise, as we must, that proportional representation means making coalition normal, further problems arise in deciding what is fair about a coalition. Nobody votes for it and on the logic of the reformists' case, it would seem that a fair coalition would have to be constructed from all the parties. In any case, before we reach that point, the reformists have in fact allowed their concerns with fairness to evaporate. If we were to take the line indicated by the reformists – that is, the line of supposing that 'fairness' is the first requirement of a system – we would be forced to the abnegation of democracy, not its fulfilment. If we choose, as they do, to stop half-way along the road, then the most we can achieve is rather little; it is only a very limited sort of fairness that might be achieved by any plausible voting reform. A little could still be worth having of course, but seeing how little is available is only the beginning. We also have to consider how much would be given up in chasing after those slight rewards.

3
THE ANTI-DEMOCRATIC
CHARACTER OF
COALITION

One of the few things on which both sides of the proportional representation debate seem to agree is that it almost surely makes coalition more likely and very probably makes it normal. Indeed, coalition is a permanent feature of government in many countries with proportional representation. The defenders of the current system think this a great disadvantage, usually because – so it is held – coalitions tend to be unstable and to give rise to weak governments. The reformists sometimes react to that by simply denying it and there are plenty of countries in which there is nothing unusual about a stable coalition. Although it is worth considering, this does not, in the end, make the most important case against proportional representation. The reformists, however, sometimes go further and claim that coalition is positively desirable, either because it forces the partners into compromise or perhaps because it makes them less confrontational or brings more points of view into the government. That view is sometimes attacked on the basis that it promotes 'fudge' in policy-making, which is certainly a possibility, but there are other, much greater, problems.

In any case, there is more to it than that. For one thing, the benefits of compromise – such as they are – are much less significant in a two-party system than they might seem in the multi-party systems typical of proportional representation. But even these concerns are only the beginning of the argument. The most important questions are about how the recurrent necessity of coalition affects the quality of democracy and it is this issue where, I suggest, the real harm proportional representation might cause can start to be seen.

WEAK GOVERNMENT

There is a long-standing argument that coalition leads to frequent changes of government but this is certainly open to challenge. The advocates of proportional representation have found plenty of examples of stable coalitions, so that the *possibility* of stability cannot reasonably be doubted. On the other hand there is an interesting reason in the logic of bargaining to expect coalitions to be unstable. Even in the simplest case of three parties, any two of which can form a majority, a problem arises from the fact that the party left out of a coalition always has an incentive to make a good offer to one of the ones in it. Consider a coalition between parties A and B, which is balanced in the sense that each has an equal number of positions in the Cabinet. Party C, which is not in the coalition, will be able to offer either of the others – say A – an arrangement in which they have more than half of the Cabinet and Party C becomes a 'junior partner', in the sense that it has a smaller share. Even as the junior partner, it is still better off than it was in opposition. However, this puts Party B in opposition and in a good position to offer Party C a deal which is better than the one Party C is getting as junior partner. That, however, puts Party A in opposition and in just the same position as Party C was at the beginning. And so it goes on.

An argument like this can only be illustrative of a certain kind of problem. We should not imagine anything quite so dramatic as daily changes of coalition partners, since all the parties involved in the negotiation, and certainly those who find their way into government, have reason to display some seriousness and consistency of purpose. They are unlikely to win future electoral support if they not only seem entirely fickle regarding their coalition partners but also stand for nothing which they are not prepared to trade and re-trade in successive rounds of negotiation. But the danger of a number of sharp changes of government and policy – with no input from the voters – is not to be dismissed, even if the complete collapse into chaos in the extreme case is unlikely.

There is another aspect to the issue of weak government. To be 'weak' does not necessarily mean 'short-lived'. In addition to that problem, it may be that they are indecisive and prone to inaction. We can easily see how this could be. Even if coalition partners are agreed on the need for action, perhaps in response to some new issue, they may not agree on what action to take. The danger would be that attempting to tackle the issue would create or expose division within the coalition and for that reason it would seem more expedient to take no action. This is one setting in which the general discipline of a single-party government can be a great asset, because it allows the leadership to take some action when it is needed. In a coalition it might be necessary to begin negotiations more or less anew in the light of whatever unexpected events occur, and with the rest of the coalition's programme underway, that might prove difficult. More or less this point was emphasised by Nouriel Roubini and Jeffrey Sachs in their study of the budgetary behaviour of coalition governments.[1] They found that countries with coalition governments tended to have larger public borrowing than did those with single-party government. Interestingly, this was not because of a general tendency of coalitions to spend too much. Rather, they said that such governments find it hard to agree on cuts when a situation demands them. Such an inability to act firmly 'during' the life of a government is, obviously, a kind of weakness which we want to avoid.

THE IDEA OF COMPROMISE

An argument often suggested is that coalition is actually desirable, because it forces the parties into co-operation and compromise and that this must be a good thing and presumably, therefore, lead to preferable outcomes. Much of the appeal of this view arises from the presumption that 'compromise' means that the resulting policy will be one of moderation. If we think of the three parties being Labour, the Liberal Democrats and the Conservatives, arranged in that order, from left to right, then any coalition would result in more centrist policies than would government by either Labour or the Conservatives alone.

If we also suppose that the voters are distributed along this left–right spectrum, then something to be said for such compromise is that it brings policy nearer to what we might call the 'centre of gravity' of the voting population. There is surely something desirable in that outcome since it would seem to be more consistent with democratic government if policies are taken from near the middle of the voters' positions.

However, there are several difficulties with this view. First, there is a very large number of policy views that are very hard to locate along a left–right spectrum. There is, for example, nothing intrinsically left or right about environmentalist positions nor about the question of how many aircraft carriers we ought to have or whether they should carry planes.[2] Nor, for that matter, is there anything left or right about whether we should adopt the alternative vote and have fixed-term parliaments.[3] Other policies have, historically, been one or the other but have come to be broadly accepted. The creation of the National Health Service may have been a decision of the left but is now widely accepted. The idea that gas and electricity companies should be privately owned and managed was an idea of the right in the 1980s but it too has ceased to be a matter of mainstream political debate. Others have at certain times been associated with either left or right but the association is not intrinsic, as we can tell from the changes that occur. For example, in 1972 the Labour Party opposed British membership of the European Economic Community but by the 1990s and certainly by the 2000s, it was hard to argue that Euroscepticism was principally a left-wing cause. Yet none of these are peripheral issues; they have all been hotly debated in British politics. Rather, the left–right spectrum is quite inadequate for describing our political culture. So, if we are to treat the idea of compromise policy seriously, it will have to be issue-by-issue compromises. Imagining a middle point on a single spectrum will not work.

There are also many issues about which it is hard even to make sense of what a compromise might be. It is all very well if we suppose that every policy is more or less like the question of whether the top rate of income tax should be forty or fifty per cent. There, a compromise is readily available, but for most issues that is not the case. What is the compromise between those who think gas companies should be publicly owned and those who think they should be in private hands? They could be partly private but that might well satisfy none of the objectives of either party. Those who oppose nuclear power would probably prefer to have fewer nuclear power stations rather than more but the point of the policy is to have none. Or how are the remaining few who wish to join the euro supposed to compromise with those who do not? In reality, 'compromise' between parties probably does not mean adopting a middle position among their various policies but simply horse-trading policy-for-policy. We have to hope that someone has an eye to the overall coherence of the package but whatever the merits of a particular deal, the idea that this process would generally make for superior policy is just a fantasy. Certainly, it does not fulfil its initial promise, because it does not result in moderation so much as simply mixture.

Even this, however, gives far too much to the case for compromise. Let us accept – contrary to reality but for the sake of the argument – that voters, policies and parties can all be more or less lined up left to right and that straightforward compromises are possible. Up to now, we have presumed that the only coalition partners come from the three major parties and while the smallest is treated as the most centrist, all coalitions must promote moderation. But why should it be like that? Let us imagine a four-party system, in which there are two large parties, one of the centre right, one of the centre left and two others, one at each extreme. The two large parties might form a coalition but in the event that either forms a coalition with the extreme party on their side, the result is to take the compromise *away* from the centre of gravity of the electorate as a whole. There would be a more centrist policy if a large party governed alone.

There is a similar case in which the coalition partner of a major party is not a conventional 'extreme' party but instead one with a narrow policy interest. There may be no way to bargain with such a party except by giving a substantial amount of ground on the particular policies that motivate them. We can easily imagine a large enough group of Scottish and Welsh nationalists pulling a much larger coalition partner into a position far from the consensus of British politics on matters of devolution or independence. (I am definitely not judging the merits of the case for independence; I am merely doubting whether the outcome of negotiations in a situation in which those favouring it happened to be in a strong position is the kind of 'compromise' that the advocates of proportional representation seem to suppose would be both beneficial *and* 'more democratic'.) Similar points could be made about the Northern Ireland parties, a larger group of Green Party members and various other parties that might happen to find themselves represented in a Parliament.

Let me say again that my point is not to seek to advance or retard the case for electoral reform by drawing attention to who might be winners or losers. The point is to challenge what I believe to be the complacent presumption of the advocates of reform that coalition means compromise and compromise means moderation, so that we can count on proportional representation to bring a government near to the centre of gravity of the views of the voters. It is *definitely not* a characteristic of coalition that it brings this effect.

AN ALTERNATIVE TO COMPROMISE

If we want to match government positions with the centre of gravity of voters' views, there is a lot to be said for a simple two-party system, as long as we make realistic assumptions about the behaviour of politicians. Political parties may once have been, as Edmund Burke's classic definition has it, 'a body of men united for promoting by their joint endeavours the national interest, upon some particular principle in which they are all agreed'.[4] But he was writing in 1770 and it is a most unrealistic view of the character of a mature party in a modern democracy. All major democratic parties should be seen primarily as organisations which exist for the purpose of contesting for power by electoral means.[5] In other words, they are not, principally, organisations which exist for the pursuit of specific ideological or policy goals. There may be elements of ideological consistency in a party's position but for the purpose of analysing and understanding how democracy works, that is not the interesting thing about them.

This view will be fiercely resisted by the party faithful of all colours. It would have to be, since it takes the meaning from their faith. It will perhaps be even more fiercely resisted by the leadership of the major parties – the party politicians and the paid party managers. For them, the idea that they are pursuing specific goals is an essential motivation of the party faithful and hence essential to the leaders' own success. The leaders must romanticise their party's history for the delight of their supporters but for our analysis of the system we need firmer ground.

THE CASE AGAINST VOTING REFORM

A party cannot be a large, successful one, with a chance of holding power, unless it has a wide appeal. So, to be in a position to win power, it must arrange to have that wide appeal. True enough, newly formed parties can have all the ideological fervour in the world; but then they are newly formed. Older parties can, if they choose, preserve a purist commitment to certain positions. But parties only come within range of winning elections when they have wide appeal.

Much of their quest to achieve that wide appeal will depend on the presentation of their leader as a suitable Prime Minister but in so far as their success is determined by their policy positions and what the other parties say about them, we should expect them to seek out popular positions. It is easy to observe that parties do not stick to losing positions, as they would if they had a true commitment to them. With few exceptions, the Conservative government that was in power from 1951 to 1964 accepted the changes made by the Labour government of 1945–51, radical though they were. Similarly, the Labour government of 1997–2010 did very little to undo the actions of the Conservative government of 1979–97, though they had opposed them fiercely when they were implemented. This last case is particularly significant because in the 1983 general election, the Labour Party said it would reverse much of what had been done by the first Thatcher government. It was attacked over this and its leaders made to seem foolish, so that in the event, it lost badly and change began immediately, through Neil Kinnock, briefly John Smith and then Tony Blair. It was a tough business because, evidently, many of the party faithful were committed to unpopular positions. But while those views controlled the party, they did not hold power. Tony Blair was rather clear about his views, saying:

> Under Neil Kinnock and John Smith we had of course broadened, deepened and become more popular, but it felt to me – and more importantly to the public – like a negotiation between us and our past. We were talking in an upbeat way, but there was a tinge of reluctance about it, a reverence for the old days that smacked of denial about how bad it had been. There was a care in speaking about the way things were that indicated an uncertainty, a lack of thorough conviction about the way things would be in the future.
>
> I wanted us to be emphatic, to be in the centre ground from belief, with passion and with the total clarity that left our past behind, not in the sense that we didn't keep the structure of our traditional beliefs, including their central foundation – the commitment to social justice – but rather that new ways of developing such foundations were needed in the modern world.[6]

In other words, while the vague objectives could stay, policy was to change completely. In case there is any doubt about it, he shortly concluded: 'So: no return to the old union laws; no renationalisation of the privatised utilities; no raising of the top rate of tax; no unilateralism; no abolition of grammar schools'.[7] This is no general list of ideas: each of these points rejects a specific commitment of the 1983 manifesto. The same general pattern is observable in the transformation brought to the Conservative Party by David Cameron. The difficulties of the Conservative Party in 1997 were rather more matters of conduct and behaviour and less of policy than was the case with Labour in 1983 but Cameron too was also taking over from others – William Hague, Iain Duncan Smith and Michael Howard – who had failed to make the party electable. He made it, at least, much more electable by rejecting the attitudes that had proved damaging.

On this theme, there is much to be learned from the much publicised, lip-read exchange between David Miliband and Harriet Harman during Ed Miliband's first speech as Labour leader. In the course of his speech, he expressed the view that the Iraq War had been a mistake and Harman applauded. David Miliband, sitting beside her, was seen to ask her why she was doing that, noting that she had voted in favour of the war. She replied, 'I'm clapping because he is the leader. I'm supporting him'.[8] To some the most interesting thing is the disagreement between the Miliband brothers; to others it says something about Harman's flexibility of mind. I would suggest it is *precisely* what we should expect – *and* we should be prepared to welcome it. When parties are seen, first and foremost, as organisations which exist for the contesting of elections and the elevation of their leaders into positions of power, reactions like Harman's are not only inevitable but necessary. How is a party to be an effective challenger for government if it does not follow its leader?

It is important to note that this kind of reaction is essential for the parties, but also for effective democracy. If the Labour Party adopted a position that gave it no chance of forming a government – say, by fighting interminably with itself over the Iraq War – it could not be an effective opposition. The absence of an effective opposition means it is no threat to the government, which is then set free from the Day of Judgment. The losers are the voters. So, while it is inevitable that politicians will take the attitude Harman did, there is nothing there to be upset about. Such a reaction is precisely what is required for effective democracy.

With this in mind we can return to the picture of voters arranged along a line from left to right. Obviously, if the voters are in more or less fixed positions, in a two-party system, the parties have a powerful incentive to move towards the middle ground. The right-wing party has no votes to gain by remaining three-quarters of the way along the line; by moving leftward it remains the party nearest to all the voters on its right but takes more of the centre ground.

Similarly, the left-wing party can be expected to move towards the right. If we take this image to its limit, we end up with two parties, side-by-side, right in the middle, one being the party of the 'left' and the other of the 'right' in only a rather nominal way. There are certainly reasons not to go this far. The most important is that successful political leadership can change the location of the 'centre' and move public opinion towards the position adopted by a party. Even so, the party ends up located in the middle ground. Despite this, and other limitations of the argument, there is no reason to deny its general importance. A pure two-party system is almost bound to drive the parties towards the middle.[9]

Although I have put this argument in terms of 'left' and 'right', we do not need to assume that issues must be treated as a package, nor that they are easily placed on that particular spectrum. The forces of electoral advantage will drive the parties to the middle ground on each issue separately. That still leaves the 'yes or no' issues – such as the euro – where it is hard to say what middle ground exists. Those cases might become fertile ground for political leadership, or failing that, we might expect to see the parties adopt whatever seems to be the more popular position with the voters. And in this notable case, this is precisely what has happened.[10]

The same tendency to seek out the voters naturally makes the major parties receptive to ideas they can present as attractive. So, the argument that coalition would bring more ideas into government seems to be just a mistake. At any point in time, there are numerous people or parties who imagine they have good ideas about things but there is no reason to suppose that those people need to be brought into a government for their ideas to be put into effect. On this point it would be interesting to know what good ideas the advocates of proportional representation think have not had a proper airing in British politics because of the inability of their advocates to work their way into a coalition government. I would guess we would have a long search to find any.

Once we see the way in which parties aspiring to government must be driven towards the centre ground, it becomes much harder to see what the real benefits of coalition might be. The case for coalition is supposed to be that it brings moderate policy. It may or may not do that, depending on the coalition, but the two-party system puts *constant* pressure on the parties to adopt acceptable positions. Clearly enough, coalition has little to offer here.

We do not have a two-party system, of course. The same line of thinking suggests that life will be hard for additional centrist parties, since it is not clear what space they can occupy. There are various things they might do: they can try to devise policies which distinguish them as different from the others – the not-quite-forgotten Liberal

Democrat commitment to adding one per cent to income tax and spending the money on education is an example.[11] Or they might adopt a relatively unpopular position on one of the 'yes or no' issues, hoping for the support of the minority. There are other cases – such as the Green Party and the UK Independence Party – where the basis of party policy is the single-minded pursuit of a narrow range of issues. Their appeal lies in their single-mindedness but were they to find themselves within range of forming a government, they would be forced to adopt a full range of policies and the same forces would drive them towards the middle ground. Straightforwardly extreme parties also might find an opening when the major parties are driven to the centre.

It is also clear that – in the terms discussed here – the two-party system has distinct advantages. A pure two-party system would normally offer us a choice between two parties, not far off being two centre parties. It is the possibility of other parties emerging that makes for the kind of coalition that drags a large party away from the centre. The emergence of more extreme and more special-issue parties can only detract from the centralising tendency of two-party competition. So, if the current British voting system makes life hard for third and smaller parties – as it does – and thereby promotes the two-party system, that is a benefit, not a cost.

HOW COALITION POLITICS HARMS DEMOCRACY

The next thing is to consider the dangers that the necessity of constant, or nearly constant, coalition creates. These flow from a simple fact: when hung parliaments are the norm and coalition comes to seem more or less inevitable, elections no longer determine who is in government. The composition of the government has to be determined *after* the election, not *by* the election. That point has been made many times by the opponents of proportional representation, often with the out-of-date annotation that the deals will be made in 'smoke-filled rooms'. The unpleasantness of the image is perhaps too often left to speak for itself, since its full ramifications point to serious damage to democracy.

The effect of proportional representation in this regard cannot be doubted. One scholar described the operation of the system in Belgium like this:

> the electorate finds itself almost totally deprived of influence on the determination of policy and on the choice of government … [voters] can, thanks to proportional representation, determine to their hearts' content the division of parliamentary seats between the numerous parties who solicit their votes. But they are practically powerless to decide upon policy or government: it is the parties which decide on these matters.[12]

While another said of Holland, 'Concerning the question of who is going to run the country, the election results give no answer'.[13]

The negotiations that determine the government do not necessarily happen straight after an election. In 1982, there was a dramatic example of the possibilities in the change of government in West Germany, which came about when the Free Democrats decided to leave their coalition with the Social Democrats and join with the Christian Democrats. There was no need for an election – the party leaders decided everything and the government changed. Another way of looking at the point is to note how some parties seem to manage to stay in government almost permanently. I have already noted (in Chapter 2) the case of the German Free Democrats being in government for eighty-six per cent of the time. But they are neither a unique nor the most extreme case. Michael Pinto-Duschinsky noted that in Italy, Japan and Switzerland, a party or group of parties remained in office continuously from the 1940s until the 1990s and in the Netherlands, one party was in government from the First World War until 1994.[14] (That beats even the record of the Communist Party of the Soviet Union, which only held power from the First World War until 1991!)

One unfortunate consequence of this could well be that parties avoid periods in opposition when they need them. While a government lasts – or a party lasts in government –

tensions build up within it. These stresses cannot be admitted, for fear of political damage, but they are inimical to effective government. A party in this position needs to go into opposition, where these problems can be admitted and one generation of leaders can be moved on to pursue the non-political ambitions and interests they are so often keen to tell us about while they are in office. The rest of the party can begin again and take the role, not of decaying government, but of credible challenger for government.

There are recent enough examples to make the case quite clear. John Major's government was, by 1997, falling apart in an unusually visible way. MPs were in open rebellion; the Prime Minister had been challenged for the leadership and had expressed frank views about some of his own backbenchers in a way he did not intend to become public, calling them 'bastards'. Although many people voted for his government at the time, it is now long enough ago for it to be uncontroversial that the Major government needed to be brought to an end in 1997 (if not sooner). Equally, and sticking to a non-partisan view, it ought to be uncontroversial that the Conservative Party of 2010 has the internal coherence and the will and capability to govern that was lacking in 1997. Realistically, that change could only have been brought about in opposition. The condition of the Labour Party in 2010 was much better than that of the Conservative Party in 1997 but even so, when they were thrown into opposition, all five of the candidates for the leadership said it needed to 'change' and a number of them revealed that they had not in fact supported the policy of the last government. Ed Miliband, as the party's new leader, declared that it had been undermined as a result of 'losing its way'.[15] Perhaps that was not quite an admission that the government needed to be brought to an end but it is not far off.

Again, therefore, the health of the system is at stake. Whatever our political views, we need a government which has the basic capability to govern and we need an opposition which is a plausible alternative government. So, we must have at least two parties which have that capability. When one party loses it through the strains of being in office, it needs to be removed. What we do not want is the possibility of its losing support but, by the construction of a coalition, remaining in power.

Another important issue is that of how voters are supposed to know what they are voting for. When coalition is all but inevitable, everyone knows that the parties which form a government must compromise. The question is what the voters, when they cast their votes, are expected to suppose about the future compromises. We have, of course, an excellent example of the problem in recent events. In the 2010 election, the Liberal Democrats promised not to raise university tuition fees and to move towards their abolition.

The coalition, however, decided they would be raised. The Liberal Democrat leadership, quite understandably said that compromise is necessary in coalition. However, Vince Cable (one of their senior MPs) went further. He told the *Politics Show* that although the manifesto had contained a 'commitment', the fact that they had not won the election meant they had not broken a 'promise' when they joined a government set on doing the opposite of what they had said.[16] There was no policy that the Liberal Democrats emphasised more than this one, so if it is not a promise, surely nothing was. The consequence is that nothing in the manifesto could be relied on by the electors, except in the event that the Liberal Democrats won the election out-right. Many people are obviously concerned and upset by that but my suggestion is that we have to accept Cable's basic outlook. The Liberal Democrats have indeed not formed a government. Compromise is necessary. It is a judgment how much and over what to compromise – and some might fault the Liberal Democrats on that – but some judgment had to be made. Naturally, that judgment had to involve abandoning parts of their policy (as it did for the Conservative Party) but there is nothing to be done about it – that is the nature of coalition.

A certain desperation is obvious in Cable's position but we must be clear what the crucial point is. It is not that politicians break promises; of course they do. Nor is it that coalition requires compromise; of course it does. The key is that coalition creates a necessity of breaking promises, and an *excuse* for it, so that the electors can never know where they are or what they are voting for. It is not so much government as *democracy* that is damaged by the inevitability of coalition.

The political parties could respond to this by saying more about their coalition plans before the election. In some countries this is quite normal. To date, the Liberal Democrats have, for the most part, tended to shy away from that, while the others have not wanted to contemplate anything less than an outright win. In any case, there is nothing that holds the parties to what they say on this issue and again we have a current example: Lord Ashdown – a former Liberal Democrat leader – specifically denied the possibility of a Liberal Democrat coalition with the Conservatives during the 2010 election campaign, saying, 'Nick Clegg cannot work with David Cameron' and 'We could not go into a coalition with the Tories, it wouldn't work'.[17] So how can the voters decide who to support?

There is also the question of how voters might retrospectively assess the parties that have come together to form a government. At election time – so I have argued – one of the keys to effective democracy is that voters can make an assessment of the government they have had. If that government has been a coalition, however, there might be serious problems. True enough, if the coalition partners were to fight a subsequent election together, defending their joint record in government, then no harm would be done. But, in that case, it would have moved towards becoming a single party and not be quite so much a 'coalition' as it had seemed. However, if at the end of the Parliament the coalition dissolves and the former partners fight the election against each other, how are the voters to assess them? There is no difficulty for the parties, nor will it be a concern for their committed supporters; they know who to vote for. But for the floating voters – those who try to decide how to vote on the merits of the case – it is of crucial importance. For the parties, promises not kept can easily enough be blamed on the need to negotiate with the other party (or parties); similarly, any failures of the government are no doubt more to do with the way the coalition partners wanted to handle things than something any party will accept as its responsibility. Nothing about that is in any way unreasonable; there is nothing to say the excuses are necessarily insincere. The problem is just that we – the voters – cannot ever be quite sure who is really to blame. That suits the governing parties because it allows them to throw sand in the eyes of the voters. But it should not suit the voters at all.

It is worthwhile to draw a contrast between coalitions and political parties. It is sometimes said that all parties are in fact coalitions, since their members do not always have exactly the same views about all the issues. Furthermore, it is said that an advantage of formal coalition would be that it would be 'open' in contrast to the concealment of differences of view typical of single-party government. This argument, however, suppresses the point that parties are not coalitions in the relevant sense. This is because they are organisations in which the members accept that they stand or fall together. When they fall, they might fight amongst themselves to find a way to appeal again to the electors; but in any case they stand or fall together. In a coalition, the parties ask to be judged separately, although they may have a joint record in government. That is the crucial difference that debilitates the voters.

Perhaps the most important consequence of coalition becoming the normal condition and elections ceasing to determine who is in government is that this threatens the abolition of the Day of Judgment. Even when voters feel they know how to vote, in all but the most extreme situations they are deprived of the opportunity to eject a party from office. Rather, most elections serve only to achieve a mild re-balancing of parliamentary forces, perhaps changing the political dynamics of the negotiations between the party leaders but always leaving it open to some part of a failed government to manoeuvre itself into the next government as well.

The proponents of proportional representation routinely say that all governments can be removed if the voters choose to remove them. In a way, that is true. If no one votes for a party, it will surely not remain in the government. That is, however, hardly a sensible way of looking at the issue; no one expects major political parties to disappear altogether. What we want – or what we want if we are wise – is a system which makes the party leaders *vulnerable* to the electorate. Proportional representation and coalition government offer a system in which they can evade our judgment.

Conclusion

We should be clear about the extent to which these arguments suggest that coalition government will necessarily be bad government. They all suggest a *danger* of bad government, whether because of the instability of the government, incoherence in its negotiated programme, inaction in the face of new developments, the lowering of a governing party's capacity after a long period in office, the inability of voters to allocate blame where it belongs, the possibility that a re-jigging of coalition will keep failures in office or simply because the Day of Judgment is avoided as governing parties become too sure of their power and fail to attend to good policy. But these are only possibilities. Coalition need not give us bad government – that just depends on the coalition.

THE CASE AGAINST VOTING REFORM

What is much clearer is the impairment of *democracy* that results from perpetual coalition. It is not merely that coalition makes it all but impossible for voters to know how to cast a vote to get the outcome they desire; it also allows the coalition partners to escape individual responsibility when it is time to assess the outgoing government. Most importantly, for democracy to be effective, parties and their leaders must face a threat of being removed from government and their fate must be determined by *voters*. If voters do not have that power, we do not have much of a democracy. But if voters are to have this power, they must be in a position to decide which parties have served them well and which have served them badly. Coalitions impair their ability to do this. Even when voters can make such a decision, political deals might keep the wrong people in office, blunting the vital democratic weapon of the Day of Judgment. To add insult to these very considerable injuries, the trick to staying in government is nothing at all to do with winning over the hearts and minds of the voters. Rather, the parties' principal plan could be to stay in office by keeping close to their parliamentary friends in other parties. Once again, the danger is the victory of the Parties over the People. If we are democrats, let us preserve as far as possible this vital piece of democracy: elections decide who governs.

4

THE INCENTIVES ON PARTIES, POLITICIANS AND VOTERS

Another issue that is all but neglected as the usual debate is conducted is the question of how proportional representation would affect the behaviour of parties, politicians and voters. The presumption seems to be that all proportional representation really means is that the Liberal Democrats would have more seats, while Labour and Conservative would have fewer. There would then be coalition but otherwise, except for a few details, it would be more or less business as usual.

This is a very poor analysis. If we decided that the result of a football match would, in future, be determined by the number of corners awarded, rather than the number of goals scored, football teams would not follow the same strategies. If we change the voting rules, the parties, politicians and voters will also behave differently. So, we must consider how the behaviour of each of these groups will change. These are obviously not separate questions, since whether political parties or individual politicians do things differently and if so, in what way, will depend on how the voters behave. Equally, how the voters behave must, at least in some cases, depend on what the parties and the politicians do.

PARTIES AND THE WHIPPING SYSTEM

Advocates of proportional representation often advance the idea that it would loosen party discipline. As I suggested in Chapter 1, a reasonable degree of party discipline can be very helpful to voters who are trying to assess their leaders but cannot be expected to make minute assessments of every speech an MP makes or vote they cast.

There should also be concern that systems of proportional representation which allow voters to choose between candidates of the same party give the candidates every incentive to try to take votes from others of their own party.

They cannot realistically attack them directly, but they can try to outbid them in making particular and extravagant promises on local matters. Consequently, candidates are driven into a parochialism that can, in the round, serve no purpose and which distracts from the problems of forming a national policy. The situation in the Republic of Ireland, which has such an electoral system, may offer an example of the kind of problem. Since that country's financial crisis, the fact that members of the Dáil (parliament) spend vast amounts of time on constituency work has – understandably – been seen as distracting them from the more important business of scrutinising national policy.[1] But of course it is the electoral system that drives them in that direction. So, while the Jenkins Commission welcomed the aspect of STV that allows voters the choice between candidates, they appear not to have considered the consequences in much depth.[2]

There is, however, another issue as to how proportional representation would affect the behaviour of the *parties* and their efforts to control their members. As Vernon Bogdanor – a most notable scholar of these things – put it:

A breach of party discipline is more serious when the government is a coalition than when it is a single-party government, since, through undermining the basis of confidence between the parties comprising the coalition, it threatens the whole *raison d'être* of an inter-party government.[3]

The natural consequence is that the parties will work harder to ensure that their MPs conform to the coalition policy. Indeed, it is also natural to take a further step, as Bogdanor did, and say that recurrent coalition would make the parties more anxious to control who stands for their party, making sure that only 'reliable' candidates are selected. Whether they would be able to do this depends on many factors but it is clear which way the pressure would be.

The Liberal Democrat rebellion over tuition fees throws up an example which might seem to contradict this idea. This is a somewhat exceptional case, both because of the very personal 'pledges' that Liberal Democrats signed on the question[4] and because the Coalition Document specifically allowed them to abstain on the issue.[5] The force of Bogdanor's point, however, relates to the response of the party machines to the recognition that coalition is the norm. It is clear that a party which is basically in the business of selling its parliamentary votes to the highest bidder will see a great advantage in ensuring that it can actually deliver those votes. Exactly how it might go about doing that is an interesting question but the idea that no effort would be made is absurd. That can only be wishful thinking on the part of the reformists. In fact we could expect to end up with candidates both drilled to vote for party policy *and* perpetually distracted by the demands of local politics.

THE EXPRESSION OF VOTER PREFERENCES

Another common claim is that proportional representation would bring an end to 'tactical voting'. Voters would be induced to vote according to their 'true preference' rather than to achieve the best practical outcome in their constituency. However, it has been mathematically shown that in any voting system where there are more than two parties, the possibility of tactical voting always exists.[6] The claim is therefore not correct.

One rather telling example of tactical voting in a country with proportional representation comes from West Germany. In 1972, the Social Democrats were hoping to form a post-election coalition with the much smaller Free Democrats. For this to happen, the Free Democrats had to poll at least five per cent of the total vote since in Germany, parties achieving less than this do not benefit from the 'proportional' system. Since it was in doubt whether this would happen, the Social Democrats asked their supporters to vote for the Free Democrats (and analysis suggests some of them did).[7] I am not sure how this can be described as a sensible system for representing voter preferences but there it is. In their discussion of tactical voting, the Jenkins Commission considered the possibility that something very much like this might happen under their proposals but dismissed it without mentioning the West German example, on the basis that neither the voters nor the parties would be able to work out the situation well enough to make use of such a possibility.[8]

To make a further assessment of these issues, we need to form some idea of how much tactical voting actually occurs in the current system, and that is not easy. As it is usually treated, the typical case in Britain is that of a Labour supporter who votes for a Liberal Democrat in the belief that this is the only practical way of preventing the election of a Conservative. This almost surely occurs to some extent and indeed Liberal Democrats will campaign on the basis that inducing such tactical voting is one of their goals. However, there are other cases that should be considered. Anyone who does not vote for a small party because it has no chance of winning is a tactical voter. The supporters of small parties who do not even have a candidate they might vote for because, having no chance of winning, no candidate stood, are in the same position.

Taking these various groups together, it is hard to know how many tactical voters there are but perhaps a partial picture may be drawn from the elections to the European

Parliament, which are conducted under a (nearly) proportional system. If it is true that this more or less eliminates tactical voting, the results might be a guide to what would happen in a proportional representation system for a Westminster election. In a parliamentary election, there are 632 seats (excluding Northern Ireland). Under a fully proportional system, any party which won 1/632 of the total votes (0.16 per cent or about 1½ votes in a thousand) would win a seat. In the last European elections, no fewer than seventeen parties (or independent candidates) reached this threshold. These are shown in Table 1, along with the approximate number of seats they would have won.

It must be admitted that this analysis is not altogether satisfactory. Voters might well express different preferences in European parliamentary elections and Westminster elections, not only because of the voting system but because of different roles of the two Parliaments. We can all speculate as to what difference this might make. My guess would be that it would affect the shares of the top four parties more than most of the rest and I do not see why it should greatly affect the number or support of the smaller ones. This is important, because many calculations of the effects of proportional representation presume that the total votes cast for the various parties in British general elections can be used to estimate how many seats would be won under a different system. However, looking at these results suggests that the

Table 1[9]

	Votes	%	Proportional allocation of seats
Conservative	4,198,394	27.9	177
UKIP	2,498,226	16.6	105
Labour	2,381,760	15.9	100
Liberal Democrats	2,080,613	13.8	88
Green Party	1,303,745	8.7	55
BNP	943,598	6.3	40
Scottish National Party	321,007	2.1	14
English Democrats	279,801	1.9	12
Christian Party "Proclaiming Christ's Lordship"	249,493	1.7	10
Socialist Labour Party	173,115	1.2	7
No2EU – Yes to Democracy	153,236	1.0	6
Plaid Cymru	126,702	0.8	5
Jury Team	78,569	0.5	3
UK First	74,007	0.5	3
Libertas	73,544	0.5	3
Jan Jananayagam	50,014	0.3	2*
Pensioners Party	37,785	0.3	2

* Ms Jananayagam was an independent and so could not in fact have taken two seats.

very small parties might gain many more votes in proportional representation. Table 1 gives some clear examples: in the general election of 2010, the BNP scored less than two per cent of the vote; in the European Parliamentary elections they scored over six per cent. In the general election, the Christian Party won just 18,000 votes – about one-fourteenth of their European election results.[10] There is no reason to think most of these parties should have benefited so much from the fact that it was a *European* election. It is much more likely the change was because the system was a (nearly) proportional one. In that case, Table 1 may give a reasonable indication of the array of parties we might expect to have under a proportional system and a picture of the results of eliminating 'tactical voting'.

Advocates of proportional representation routinely make two contrasting responses to this kind of point. One is that the proposal is not for *full* proportionality and this kind of proliferation of parties would be prevented by the fine details of the system. Indeed, most actual systems of 'proportional representation' do not result in representation for the smallest parties. The simplest method is simply to define a 'threshold' level of support that parties must reach before benefiting from the 'proportionality' of the system. In British debates, a popular figure has been five per cent, the figure used in Germany. The top six parties in Table 1 would reach this level. In another variation, the threshold would not apply to the country as a whole but separately to regions. This would mean that the Scottish Nationalists and Plaid Cymru would reach five per cent if Scotland and Wales were treated as 'regions'. The Jenkins Commission did not achieve the effect in this way but they estimated that their proposals would mean that parties would have to reach about eleven per cent before benefiting from the system.[11]

There is an obvious commonsense reason for these sorts of rules but it is less clear how they can be accommodated within what is otherwise presented as an argument of principle. If proportional representation is about the demand for 'fair votes', why would that not extend to Jan Jananayagam, should she choose to stand in a Westminster election? What principle says Wales should be a 'region', so that Plaid Cymru passes a threshold, if the more popular Socialist Labour Party is not to be so favoured? Apart from that kind of issue, it is surely the case that if it is not quite a farce, it is certainly a curiosity that making proportional representation palatable even to its advocates requires the introduction of devices *specifically* to prevent it delivering proportionality. Certainly these sorts of proposals make it look more and more as if the real case is not one for proportionality that happens to result in more Liberal Democrat MPs but rather that it is simply a device to redistribute MPs between the parties currently represented in the House of Commons. There does not seem to be any principled reason for regarding the present system as 'unfair' that would not apply equally to one that treated parties scoring over eleven per cent in a radically different way from those scoring less, although, obviously, the Liberal Democratic Party would be the beneficiary.

On the other hand, the second response that is encountered is entirely different. It can readily be summarised as: 'That's democracy!' Although we might not like the result a system throws up, if we are committed to democracy we ought to be happy to live with it. That clearly has principle behind it and is, in its way, a perfectly proper response. So this table, in itself, cannot possibly make an argument for or against proportional representation. Perhaps there should be seventeen parties (and four or five more from Northern Ireland) in the House of Commons.

WHICH PARTIES EXIST?

The difficulty with the 'That's democracy' view lies elsewhere. That response to the problem posed by Table 1 seems to presume that we are more or less compelled to accept whatever outcome a democratic election throws up. There are two reasons that cannot be accepted. First is the notorious and obvious point that democracies can do unacceptable things and if they do, they are not made acceptable by the mere fact that a democracy did it. A mad democracy could vote to exterminate blue-eyed babies but it would not make it the right thing to do.[12] In addition to this, there is also a much more subtle point about how the form a democracy takes can affect not only the decisions it reaches but even what it is that the people *want* to happen. In the current context, this arises from the question of how our choice of voting system will affect the behaviour of parties and how that will affect the behaviour of voters.

The usual criticism of the current system – that it inhibits small parties – is by no means all bad news. Put slightly differently, it could be said that it encourages smaller groups to form themselves into larger parties. For that reason, if we were to change to a proportional representation system, existing large parties might split. Under the current system, this would mean the new, smaller parties would win very few seats, because the vote would be divided among them. However, under a properly proportional system, that would not be a concern – each of the new, smaller parties could expect representation appropriate to its share of the vote. Another possibility is that wholly new parties would be created. In that case, the danger and the expectation would be that these would be parties dedicated either to the pursuit of a narrow range of issues or the representation of a narrow group of voters. We can imagine many kinds of such parties. One example might be regionalist parties, with the central policy aim of bringing advantages to a certain region, or certain social groups might also create parties. In 2003, a Member of the Scottish Parliament was elected for the 'Scottish Senior Citizens Unity Party'.[13] Other groups might seek to be represented in the same kind of way. There might be candidates from the Taxpayers Alliance (a lobby group for low taxes), or private car drivers wanting more roads built, presenting themselves as a counterweight to the Green Party in the process. If English regions or major cities did not produce parties, the various groups of English nationalists might. There are also the parties which are not currently represented in the House of Commons but which contested the European elections: UKIP, the BNP, Proclaiming Christ's Lordship, Socialist Labour, Jury Team, Libertas and all the rest of them. The possibilities are limited mostly by imagination, since a group that could organise itself sufficiently well would find voters it appealed to. To be clear, the question is not whether groups such as senior citizens are entitled to have their interests properly weighed up in Parliament. Of course they are. The issue is whether a system which promotes a proliferation of parties of relatively narrow interests or very specific objectives is a good system. To answer that, we have to consider how parties would behave in this situation.

If we had so many parties, government would require coalition, and presumably multi-party coalition. I have already suggested that is undesirable, but when we think specifically about narrow-interest parties in coalition, there are further problems. To explore the issues we might think of one particular category of party – regionalist parties. It must be a possibility that there would be such parties. For example, in versions of proportional representation which create large, multi-member constituencies covering whole cities there could easily be candidates whose manifesto would not amount to much more than putting their city at the top of all priority lists. The right people in a city with a strong sense of identity and friendly local media might well be strong candidates and, to be elected, they would only need to win a sufficient share of the vote. If such a group could achieve electoral success and if it found itself in an environment where multi-party coalition was the norm, there seems to be no real reason that it should not achieve its objectives, at least up to a point.

Even in our current system, regionalist policies are sometimes adopted for more or less purely party-political reasons. No doubt all MPs take an interest in promoting their region but the most notorious piece of policy formed on such a basis is surely the decision to build the Humber Bridge in 1966. The government, which at the time had a majority of three, announced its decision just a few days before the Hull North by-election. The bridge embodies some notable architecture but over the succeeding decades has remained a financial disaster.[14] On the other hand, I take it that no one is surprised that the government won the by-election.

As this example shows, the danger is not that regionalist parties would invent a whole new kind of politics. Rather, it is that these parties would find that the entire reason for their existence lay in their pursuit of sectional goals. Those who voted for such parties might well be voting for a fair deal but the careers of the politicians would depend on their delivering identifiable benefits for the interest group they represent. For them, everything would depend on this narrow success and any coalition which needs their support will have only as much room for manoeuvre as that permits.

The narrowness of such parties' concerns means that these are not parties which are likely to engage in the horse-trading of policy for policy. They only want one thing: a benefit for whatever interest they are representing. When they get that, they can go along with other policies but if they cannot, they are unlikely to support anyone else. The consequence of this is apparent – a proliferation of such parties cannot be conducive to the formation of nationally orientated policy. At least with an ordinary coalition, where policy is traded for policy, there is some hope of the result having a reasonable breadth of appeal. But not in this case. On the other hand, such parties are unlikely to produce much overall benefit – in the end they would probably turn out to be fighting with each other over the allocation of public expenditure.

For the reason that there are no overall benefits from this development, there is a particular interdependence in the incentives to create or vote for such parties. I imagine that as things are, most people feel little temptation to support a special-interest or regionalist party. The issue, however, might be what reason there is to support one when other regions already have such parties. Those regions, we may suppose, would be benefiting from the existence of those parties and the benefits they receive must come at the expense of regions without such parties. Consequently, each voter's incentive to support such a party depends very much on the general prevalence of such parties. As a result it is much more likely that they will grow slowly than that they will suddenly appear. Even in the present system, we can see a slow growth of English nationalism, emphasising the idea of an English Parliament, and this is not – even by their own account – unrelated to the success of the Scottish Nationalists. The English version is not at all shy of saying that England suffers through the payment of unfair amounts of money to Scotland and that this should be corrected.[15] Why should we not see the same thing at the regional level?

From one point of view, these things offer simply one more idea of the dangers of proportional representation. That system is an invitation to interest groups to organise themselves into parties. From another point of view, how-ever, they also reveal the naïvety of the idea that voting systems are merely ways for *translating* voter preferences into outcomes and appealing to 'that's democracy' when things go wrong. Here we can see that the choice of the voting system is itself one of the things which *creates* prefer-ences. This makes it inescapable that we have to choose the *kind* of democracy we want. While we have a voting system which makes life very hard for small parties, there will be few such parties and those that exist will generally achieve little. Choose a voting system which promotes such parties and everything changes, so that eventually it could become a practical necessity of political life to campaign in that kind of way. That cannot be a demand of 'fair votes'.

ELECTORAL BEHAVIOUR OF PARTIES AND CANDIDATES

The divisiveness of such an arrangement of parties should be apparent but this is only the beginning of the problem. Further issues arise from the question of how such parties would be expected to campaign during an election or con-duct themselves generally. This question received a classic treatment from one of the great analysts of party systems – Maurice Duverger – in 1954.[16] He distinguished parties with what he called 'the majority bent' from those without it. Those with it, he said, are those with realistic prospects of forming a single-party government. That guides their policy commitments, because they are always aware that they may be called upon to implement them – they face, as he said, the 'test of realisation'. If such a party is elected and it has made promises it cannot keep, it is found out and can expect an electoral penalty.[17]

On the other hand, parties without the majority bent know they will never be in a position to implement their programme except in circumstances in which they negotiate a coalition agreement and, of necessity, compromise with their partners. For them, excuses can always be made about broken promises: the manifesto is never a real plan of action but at most a place from which to begin negotiations to form a coalition. They face no test of realisation and, since they have excuses, are much better placed to avoid a penalty when they are unable to implement their programme. Furthermore, Duverger argued, while campaigning these parties are 'led into demagogy' by the system. Nothing limits the demands they can make but in making them, they create hopes and convince their own followers of the importance of what they are demanding, so that, after the election, disappointment must follow. As Duverger put it, this rhetoric will 'stir up militant members who then refuse to be cooled down'.[18]

Again, the Liberal Democrats and their position on university tuition fees leap to attention. It is not only that a manifesto cannot be binding on a party in coalition. There is much more to it than this. The *Guardian* revealed that the Liberal Democrats had already planned to abandon part of their policy before the election.[19] Among the leaders of the party it was not only recognised that it was merely a negotiating position but it was also a position from which they had specific plans to retreat quickly. Considering the emphasis that was put on the policy, it is hard to escape the impression that one objective was to excite likely supporters of the Liberal Democrats during the election. There could hardly be a clearer case of a small party inflating the expectations of what it took to be a core group of voters with no prospect of their ever being implemented. Just as Duverger might have expected, after the event, the disappointed expectations were made visible by student riots.

It may or may not be appropriate to condemn the Liberal Democrats over their promises but that is not the point. The point is to understand the incentives that operate within parties that lack the majority bent. They face a crucial political judgment; how to create the strongest appeal to those who *might* vote for them, in circumstances in which they know they will not be the sole party forming a government. The judgment the Liberal Democrats made was, evidently, that their promises over tuition fees would attract support and that would make a worthwhile difference to their objective of sharing in government. Once in government, they tell us that they cannot implement the policy because they are not governing alone. The lesson is clear: we should not want to create a system in which most or even all parties are in the position of having little chance of governing alone, so that this kind of judgment is the one always facing them.

Alongside Duverger's emphasis on the making of expansive promises to those who might be excited by them lies another technique which is likely to serve party interests. This technique is to encourage the members of the group it seeks to represent to think of themselves as *primarily* members of that group. They will be invited to put aside their Conservatism, their support for the Labour Party, their Liberal Democracy, their environmentalism, their desire to see Britain leave the European Union or whatever it may be and to vote for the party which represents *their group*. Successful or not and irrespective of what policies the party might adopt – policies which might in every way be respectful of both the interest of the wider community and the importance of maintaining the common bonds of society – the whole business would be thoroughly divisive. Again this calls into question the understanding of the Jenkins Commission. They welcomed the idea that proportional representation would lead to a greater representation of ethnic minorities in Parliament – and there is nothing wrong with the sentiment – but they presumably did not consider that it might come about through the creation of ethnic minority parties which could achieve electoral success by emphasising the divisions between their group and the rest of society.

RECONSIDERING THE TWO-PARTY SYSTEM

In the light of these considerations, we can once more reflect on the virtues of the two-party system. In Chapter 3, I observed that two parties must feel a powerful pull towards the centre ground and suggested that this made the apparent desirability of 'compromise' rather questionable, particularly when we do not know between whom the compromise will be struck. We can now go further. In a multi-party system, the parties are faced with the constant problem of preparing for coalition. They present negotiating positions to the electors but in the nature of the thing they cannot say what compromises they will be prepared to make, since this would destroy their bargaining position. Deception and disappointment are therefore inevitable. To the extent that a party knows it will not govern alone and can therefore always find an excuse for abandoning its manifesto, the exaggeration of promises will only be greater.

In a two-party system, the parties are always preparing for government. Each party hopes to form a government and knows it will be judged on its record. This may not keep them entirely honest in the promises they make but it certainly creates limits to how far they will go. Each party's programme, too, can be scrutinised and criticised by the other party on the basis that it is an actual proposal as to what is to be done, not a starting point for negotiation. The crucial political judgments that *these* parties make must involve the question of whether they can actually implement their proposals. It is also essential that their programmes are acceptable to a wide group of voters, not merely that they enthuse a few. This, surely, is the way we want our parties to behave and this is the way they are pushed by the opportunity of single-party government. Most importantly, the parties are also forced into seeking wide appeal. They are *not* trying to shore up a limited support to gather enough seats to make a play for a share in coalition; they are trying to *win*. If a party is to do that, it has no option but to seek a breadth of appeal that would be far beyond minor parties. The idea of the Jenkins Commission that our system has a natural tendency to divide rather than unite is bizarre.

Parties may or may not succeed in making themselves appealing to a broad range of voters but the political rewards are considerable and we can see that they try rather hard. In defeat and disarray the major parties sometimes appear to be narrow class-based parties but they are not forming governments at those times, and nor are they attractive. When they emerge from such a period it is a different story and surely notable that the two most successful leaders of recent times – Margaret Thatcher and Tony Blair – succeeded *precisely* because they broadened their party's appeal beyond anything that could be construed as a narrow class base.

As it happens, there is a more recent, perfectly formed, example, albeit on a smaller scale, of the same phenomenon. It arose during the debate over child benefit, in October 2010. The Prime Minister, David Cameron, said that cutting child benefit from those earning more than £44,000 was the 'right thing to do'.[20] In response, Yvette Cooper, Labour's Work and Pensions spokesperson said – and note the expression 'middle incomes' – 'George Osborne and David Cameron obviously don't understand what it means for families on middle incomes' to lose this benefit.[21] Ed Miliband reached out further, saying that even millionaires should be entitled to claim the benefit.[22] Whatever you make of the merits of the case, it is not class war.

Conclusion

There is no particular arrangement of things which we can label as 'democracy', conveniently identified so that we can, if we want to, move closer until we reach it. No one can say what is a fair distribution of seats in Parliament and from that deduce what voting system is 'most democratic'. The reason is that we have to know the voting system before we can discuss what voters' preferences might be. Party preferences cannot exist until we know what parties there are. We have to know how the parties conduct themselves and how they make their appeal to the voters. And we cannot know these things unless we already have a voting system.

In part, this makes for another strand of the argument that 'fairness' is not a useful concept but there are other points. First, once again the advocates of proportional representation are more or less forced to accept certain elements of the case against it. Once we realise that there is a perfectly realistic chance of there being seventeen mainland parties in Parliament – and presumably more, as more and more groups see the opportunities – even the advocates of proportional representation turn against it. In doing so they lose even the partial appeal to fairness that is held to be the central aspect of their case. Second, we are forced to recognise another way in which 'democracy' is not only imperfect but imperfectible. We can all see the dangers that follow from the establishment of parties that appeal to special groups. We need to recognise that none of us is immune to that appeal. If enough other people are voting for special interest parties, it could be no more than self-preservation to do so oneself. Those who say 'That's democracy' and walk away from the problem have presumably not understood it. It would not be 'democracy'. It would be merely one possible democracy, and a very poor one.

THE INCENTIVES ON PARTIES, POLITICIANS AND VOTERS

We can choose what kind of democracy we can have. The outcome of the arguments I have considered in this chapter is that by choosing the electoral rules we go a long way towards determining the behaviour and positioning of the parties. And by determining those things, we go a long way to determining not only the *degree* to which we are democratic but also the *character* of our democracy, whether it is one based on parties seeking to advance particular interests by dealing with others similarly embarked on advancing other interests or one based on parties competing with each other in seeking to govern on the basis of broad support for a national ambition.

5

THE CASE AGAINST THE ALTERNATIVE VOTE

The alternative vote is not, of course, a proportional system. In the version which has been proposed for Britain, voters would have the option of ranking the candidates (in single-member constituencies) so that they could state which was their first choice, which their second and so on. In counting the votes, only the first preferences would initially be considered. If one of the candidates has more than half of these, that candidate would be elected. If not, the candidate with the smallest number of first preferences would be eliminated. The ballot papers of those who voted for that candidate would then be inspected to see whether the voters gave a second preference and if so, for whom. These second preferences are then added to the score for the appropriate candidates and another check would be made to see whether anyone has more votes than all the other candidates combined. If anyone does, that candidate is elected and the process stops. If not, the one who then has the smallest number of votes is eliminated and that candidate's supporters again have their vote transferred to their next choice. Eventually, the contest would come down to the last two candidates and at this point the one who has accumulated the most votes is the winner.

This system, or a close relative, is used fairly frequently in electing a single person to some role, such as the president of a country or the leader of a political party. In such cases, it has certain significant merits. The Labour leadership election of 2010 provided a kind of example, although complicated by the fact that Labour Trade Union members, party members and MPs all vote separately. However, the point is clear enough. In the first count, David Miliband, was the most popular candidate but as the bottom candidates were eliminated, more of their votes went to Ed Miliband, so that in the end he overtook his brother. Had the Labour Party been electing its leader in the manner of the current British parliamentary elections, David would have won; doing it in the manner of the alternative vote, Ed was the winner.

In the light of this sort of outcome, it is sometimes said – with some justice, although not quite accurately – that the current British system elects the 'most liked' candidate, whereas the alternative vote elects the 'least disliked'. We could probably make a case about which is the better system for electing a party leader, a national president, a city's mayor or the winner of the Oscar for best actress. However, for electing a Parliament of 600 or 650 members the alternative vote a deeply flawed method, for a variety of reasons.

One source of commentary to this effect is the considerable volume of criticism directed at it by advocates of proportional representation, even though a number of them now support it. Quite apart from Nick Clegg and his 'miserable little compromise', almost any of the prominent British proponents of proportional representation can be quoted to damn it. For example, Enid Lakeman rejected it, saying:

> Results under this system are as unrepresentative as those of a British general election. They vary from the comparatively mild distortion of the 1966 Australian House of Representatives election (a large parliamentary majority for the Liberal-Country Party alliance with a tiny popular majority) to the extreme exaggeration of the 1948 Alberta election (a clean sweep for Social Credit with 58 per cent of the total vote) and the absurdity of Victoria in 1967 when the Liberals, with fewer first preference votes than Labour, secured nearly three times as many seats.[1]

Samuel Finer quickly dismissed it as 'capricious in its results'.[2] The Hansard Commission – one of the major enquiries into proportional representation in the 1970s – said that it would not prevent 'flagrant minority rule'.[3] The Jenkins Commission favoured a two-part system, in which *some* MPs would be elected by the alternative vote and others by another mechanism but noted clearly that the alternative vote alone was not an acceptable option. They said (calling the existing British system 'first past the post' – FPTP):

> AV on its own suffers from a stark objection. It offers little prospect of a move towards greater proportionality, and in some circumstances, and those [like] the ones which certainly prevailed at the last election and may well do so for at least the next one, it is even less proportional than FPTP.[4]

Vernon Bogdanor wrote that the alternative vote and similar systems 'do not achieve and indeed do not purport to achieve, a proportional relationship between votes and seats'.[5] It is not a good start.

SOME PARTICULAR DANGERS OF THE ALTERNATIVE VOTE

Any voting system can throw up anomalies and uncomfortable results. We can never escape that. So the fact that the alternative vote has some unfortunate effects is nothing surprising but they can be both severe and disturbing.

In Chapter 2, I raised the possibility of a three-way vote between options square, triangle and circle with these voter preferences:

Group 1 consists of 100 people who rank them square – triangle – circle

Group 2 consists of 150 people who rank them triangle – circle – square

Group 3 consists of 200 people who rank them circle – square – triangle

I noted that circle is the most popular option in terms of both first preferences and first and second preferences combined but that if the vote is conducted by a sequence of head-to-head contests and circle has to face triangle, then circle loses. Another way of looking at it that gets to the same place is to think of the vote happening in the manner of the alternative vote. In that case, looking at the first preferences, the tally would be:

Square: 100
Triangle: 150
Circle: 200

None of the options has more than half the votes, so the lowest one – square – is eliminated. Those who voted for square then have their second preferences counted. Since all the Group 1 people have triangle as their second choice, the vote on the second round would be:

Triangle: 250
Circle: 200

And triangle is the winner. We might also note that in this case, 300 people prefer square to triangle whereas only 150 prefer triangle to square. So it is not even true that the alternative vote means a winning candidate must be preferred to each of the others.

That does a great deal of damage even to the idea that the winner must be the 'least disliked'. This is bad enough but we can see a worrying result from an even simpler example. Here, a voter can help the candidate they favour to be elected by voting for someone else. Suppose on first preferences Candidate A scores 100, Candidate B scores 110 and Candidate C scores 170. Go on to suppose that the second preferences of those who vote for A are overwhelmingly for B, whilst the second preferences of those who vote for B are overwhelmingly for C. In this case, if the election runs to form, A will be eliminated and the votes will go to B, who will win. Now suppose some of the C voters choose to give their *first* preference to A. If A can be moved into second place, then B will be eliminated. B's votes will then go to C, who will win.

This is a kind of tactical voting. While it might be said that it is a slightly more complicated operation than other, more familiar kinds, it is also more disturbing. Tactical voting under the existing system involves voters accepting that their candidate cannot win and so voting for whoever they regard as the best of the candidates who might win. In a way, that is just what they would do if their most favoured candidate did not stand. In the example above, people vote for a candidate they do not want because this *helps* their favoured candidate win. If there is an objection to tactical voting, this case surely goes deeper than the familiar one.

A similar point could be made about voters whose preferences change. In the case above, if candidate C were to make a bad speech the day before the vote and so lose some supporters to A, the result might be that C is elected instead of B! Surely bad speeches which lose support ought to damage a candidate's changes of winning, but under the alternative vote they might not.[6]

Another concern arises from the differential treatment of second (and subsequent) choices. In a three-cornered contest, those who vote for the third-placed candidate have their second choices counted. However, the second choices of the other losing candidate are never counted. Consider this close-run thing: Candidate A scores 201 votes, Candidate B 200 votes and Candidate C 199 votes. Let us suppose that the second preferences of Candidate C split 98 to A and 101 to B, making the final vote Candidate A 299 and Candidate B 301. B wins. But on any basis, it was close.

What if it turns out that the second preferences of those who voted first for A were *all* for C? In that case, had A been eliminated, C would have beaten B by 400 to 200 – a substantial margin.

This situation holds a kind of unfairness. Although A is, like C, a losing candidate, those who voted for A never have their second preferences taken into account. If they were taken into account, it would make it look very much as if, all told, C was a more popular candidate than B. Why should it be that C-voters have their second preferences counted, but A-voters do not? (We could ask about the B-voters' second preferences – perhaps they all go to C as well.) As Lord Alexander put it: 'the result would be different depending on which horse was second and which was third over Becher's Brook first time round. This seems to me too random to be acceptable'.[7] So why is the alternative vote a fair system?

A particularly serious manifestation of this problem can arise at the national level when there is one party which is clearly the middle party, so that it attracts a high proportion of second preferences from both of the other two parties. Suppose it tends to be that where the Top party is in first place, Middle is second but where Bottom is in first place, Middle tends to be third (and Top tends to be second). In the seats where Top is initially in first place, Bottom is eliminated and Middle gains a large number of second preferences, so that it stands a chance of overtaking Top and winning the seat. Where Bottom is initially in first place, it is Middle that is eliminated after the first count and the Middle votes are split between Top and Bottom, so that Bottom can expect to stay in the lead. The result is that it is much harder for Top candidates to win than Bottom candidates. It could be that Top and Bottom start out with exactly the same number of votes across the country as a whole and are initially in first place in exactly the same number of seats but Bottom ends up winning more, not because of any preferences amongst the voters for Bottom over Top but just because it happened that Middle was in second place in the seats where Top was strong. That would be a dismal outcome, all the more so if the point is really to achieve 'fair votes'.

Nor is there any shortage of actual election outcomes using the alternative vote which ought to be thoroughly unsatisfactory to the supporters of proportional representation. There are those cited by Enid Lakeman in the quotation above and others since she wrote. Two of the most notable come from the Australian elections to the House of Representatives in 1993 and 1990. In 1993, the Australian Labor Party won fifty-four per cent of the seats, as against the Liberal-National coalition's forty-four per cent but it had polled only forty-five per cent, as against their forty-four per cent. In 1990, even more dramatically, the ALP won fifty-three per cent of the seats with thirty-nine per cent of the votes. The Democrats, with eleven per cent, won no seats. We could, truthfully, say that neither of these outcomes was much more dramatic than the kind of thing that happens with the existing British system. However, if the *point* of the change is 'fair votes', we must surely expect better returns than this system delivers. It is perhaps no surprise that in Australia – the only major country currently using the alternative vote for national elections – there are significant signs of discontent. A 2010 opinion poll found that most voters want to abandon it and switch to the British system.[8]

Attempts to simulate the result of British elections under different voting systems also raise alarm. One thorough and careful study by a group of very reputable political scientists estimated that had the alternative vote been operating in 1997, when Tony Blair won a very large majority, it would have been even bigger. Labour's majority would have been 213 rather than the 169 it actually achieved although, of course, he only had a minority of the vote. The Conservatives, who were in any case *under*-represented relative to their share of the vote in that Parliament, would have fared even worse.[9]

One advocate of the alternative vote has dismissed these kinds of results. Peter Kellner – a widely read political journalist and commentator – said in 1998:

> AV is likely to produce the kind of distortion that occurred last year only when one of the two major parties is exceptionally unpopular. In such circumstances, the distortion will serve to reinforce the majority wish of the electorate.

> I cannot conceive of circumstances when AV-induced dis-
> tortion would undermine the majority wish.[10]

It is an interesting view that it would have been unimportant if Blair's majority had been even greater but, more importantly, Kellner has missed an important possibility; one which, as it happens, was highlighted by other evidence to the Jenkins Commission provided by an expert panel chaired by David Butler. The panel hypothesised that all Conservative and Labour supporters would give their second preference to the Liberal Democrats and considered two possible scenarios. In scenario A, the Conservatives are just short of fifty per cent in half the seats and Labour in the other half; in each case the other major party comes third and the Liberal Democrats, on twenty-six per cent, are in second place in every seat. So we have, in half the seats, Conservative forty-nine per cent, Lib Dem twenty-six per cent and Labour twenty-five per cent. In the other half, it is the same thing, except that Labour and Conservative change places. The result is that the Liberal Democrats win *every* seat, since the third party voters all switch to them, giving them fifty-one per cent. In the Butler Committee's scenario B, there is a very slight change in the numbers. The leading party in each seat now has fifty-one per cent and the third-placed party has twenty-three per cent. The Liberal Democrats have the same twenty-six per cent. In this case, the first-placed party has more than half, so it wins. Half the seats go to Labour, half to the Conservatives, and the Liberal Democrats, although their vote is unchanged, now have no seats at all![11]

The difference between the two outcomes – and its absurdity – is striking, but scenario A also shows the seriousness of Kellner's error. Although the Butler example was exaggerated, the general nature of the problem is that, in a three-party contest, a party that can come a good second in more than half the seats, and pick up a large enough number of second preferences, can win an overall majority whilst being clearly *third*-placed in the overall vote of first preferences. (In a four-party contest, it could even come fourth in overall votes and win a majority; and similarly for larger numbers.) Even if it does not win an actual majority, it could be vastly over-represented and have more seats from fewer votes than each of the other parties. One response to that might be that the Liberal Democrats do not currently seem to be in a sufficiently strong position for that to happen. However, that is no response at all if we are trying to design a system. All it really takes for this kind of problem to come to life is for the party that most voters see as the compromise party to do sufficiently well in a large enough number of seats; and that, clearly, is not impossible. So one of the problems with the alternative vote is that it raises the possibility of the truly bizarre outcome of a party that was third-placed or a distant second finding itself in a majority government. That surely would be a catastrophe for democratic legitimacy.

THE CASE AGAINST VOTING REFORM

The general problem that the alternative vote threatens a much worse disproportionality of outcome than the present system was precisely the point that Ben Bradshaw MP advanced when explaining his objection to that system:

> The reason I've never supported AV is that it would have given us an even bigger majority in 1997 and it would have given the Tories an even bigger majority in 1983 and probably 1987 as well.[12]

Bradshaw, strangely, is now the head of the Labour 'Yes to AV' campaign.[13]

It is also important to consider how the introduction of the alternative vote would be likely to affect the behaviour of the parties. It is sometimes said that since the parties will be keen to attract the second preference of those who vote for losing parties, this will cause them to campaign in a less confrontational way.[14] As I have observed, if what that means is that the parties will cease to find fault with each other and, in particular, the Opposition will cease to find fault with the Government, then however relaxing it might seem, it will debilitate democracy. The voters are in no position to find out and assess every detail of Michael Gove's plans for schools or to decide whether Philip Hammond's plan to spend £8 billion on investment in railways whilst raising fares is worth the money or not. We need to have both a Government that wants to persuade us that it is right and an Opposition that will provide us with an alternative point of view. A 'non-confrontational' politics, in which the parties are more concerned to emphasise their similarities than their differences, cannot deliver this. Any system which encourages the parties to take such an approach amounts to an invitation to them to engage in a conspiracy of silence about the defects of each other's policy. We may not welcome every aspect of the barracking that goes on but we need the confrontation. Without it, democracy is the loser.

THE CASE BEING MADE BY THE 'YES' CAMPAIGN

Why would anyone advocate the alternative vote? It is not a proportional system and has no claim to being one. It is a system which all the principal advocates of proportional representation in Britain have rejected. Yet it is now the focus of 'fair votes' campaigns.

At the time of writing (3 January 2011), the website of 'Yes to fairer votes' – the campaign organisation for the alternative vote – gave three reasons for voting for the alternative vote:

> MPs will need to secure at least 50% of the vote to be certain of winning, not just the 1 in 3 that can currently put them in power. They'll need to work harder and go further

to get – and keep – your support. They'll have to appeal to more people in the communities they seek to represent, because doing just enough won't be enough any more.

Second, forget tactical voting – just pick the candidate you really want to win. But if your favourite doesn't win you can still have a say. It's as easy as 1, 2, 3...

And third, too many MPs have 'safe seats' or jobs for life and the expenses crisis showed us just where that culture can lead. Now you can help end that culture of complacency.

It is not an impressive list. Starting with the issue of safe seats, literally hundreds of MPs have more than half the vote in their constituencies, so their seats presumably will still be safe.[15] Some safe seats will even become *more* safe. Take Bermondsey and Old Southwark, for example. The result of the 2010 election was:

Simon Hughes, Liberal Democrat	21,590
Val Shawcross, Labour	13,060
Loanna Morrison, Conservative	7,638
Various others in total	2,363

Simon Hughes has been an MP since 1983 and his seat could surely be called safe, since although he did not win fifty per cent of the vote, his lead over his nearest rival is nearly twenty per cent. Under the alternative vote, once the minor parties were eliminated, the Conservative candidate would go next and Hughes's final majority would presumably be even bigger. How is that system addressing any problem about jobs for life?

Even beyond that, we might wonder what the problem is. Although the bogey of safe seats is a routine target, their existence is not an unmixed curse. For better or worse, in Britain we form our government from Members of Parliament (not all countries have Cabinet ministers who are also elected representatives). Under this arrangement, there is surely an advantage in there being opportunities for those likely to serve in a government being elected by constituencies which do not require their full-time attention. No doubt there are costs in that arrangement but a situation in which the whole of the Cabinet should be perpetually concerned about their own re-election would hardly result in good management of the nation's affairs.

We should also note that in extreme cases, even safe seats can change hands, as the defeat of the Conservative candidate Michael Portillo in 1997 memorably showed. Much more than this, the suggestion that if a seat is safe for a party that gives the MP a job for life is simply not true. There is no better illustration of why it is false than what happened after the expenses scandal. Following the scandal over MPs' expenses claims, dozens of MPs were instructed not to stand in the election. Yet others – *The Times* suggested as many as 200 – quit because of public anger.[16] Some who still stood were defeated; notable among them the former Home Secretary, Jacqui Smith.[17] The urgency with which the parties set about preventing these individuals standing is a remarkable and clear instance of the *parties* reacting to the pressure of public opinion over this kind of issue, just as they do over policy matters.

Moving to the second supposed benefit of the alternative vote, the instruction to 'forget' tactical voting is all very well but as the example on page 115 and the discussion of the German election on page 89 show, opportunities for it remain under the alternative vote. As I pointed out in Chapter 2, there are *no* voting systems which are free of such opportunities. The point that tactical voting is always a possibility has been a commonplace of discussions of voting systems for years, including introductory ones.[18]

The remaining point at least has the advantage of containing an element of truth. It is not precise, because if voters do not state further preferences, a candidate can be elected on fewer than half the votes. But beyond that, the strength of the point is very dubious. The effect of the system is to favour candidates to whom few voters greatly object. As the example on pages 114–5 shows, a candidate can win despite the fact that another candidate is preferred by more voters. In any case, and probably much more importantly, general elections are neither local popularity nor unpopularity contests; they are the occasions on which we elect a government. We could imagine a version of the alternative vote where the national total of votes for each party determines the order of elimination of the parties. In that version, in 2010, all the small parties and then the Liberal Democrats would have been eliminated in *every* constituency and the final vote would have come down to a choice between Labour and Conservative. That is not what is being offered; the proposal is that in each constituency the least popular candidate should be eliminated until a winner is found. That is a very different thing.

In terms of bringing together a Parliament, the alternative vote seems to offer neither the advocates of the present system nor the advocates of proportional representation (proper proportional representation) what they want. In all probability, it would result in the election of more Liberal Democrats. In seats where this party is currently second to one of the other parties, they would have a chance of overtaking the current winner with second preference votes. For that reason, in circumstances like those of the present, it certainly makes hung parliaments and coalitions more likely and we may expect all the adverse consequences discussed in Chapter 3. On the crucial question of the ease and possibility of dismissing a government – its susceptibility to the Day of Judgment – the alternative vote creates a very real danger. The compromise candidate, which it favours, might be a very hard candidate to remove because the opponents of that candidate are, in the nature of the system, split into at least two camps.

We face a potential trap here in presuming that the only cases that matter are ones in which the circumstances are more or less like those prevailing today. As things are in Britain, with the Liberal Democrats as the third party, there is little prospect of them forming a government alone. With the alternative vote, either the Conservative or Labour Party might be able to form a government and *might* be able to replace each other. If so, both would be subject to the Day of Judgment. The alternative vote makes coalition more likely, so such cases might not be normal, but they would remain possible.

However, if we think of circumstances changing so that either the Liberal Democrats became a party that could govern alone or one of the other parties came to be seen as the compromise party, things would be different. A compromise party government might lose *first preference* votes to the other parties but a number of these might still be expected to return to it as second preference votes. This point can be illustrated by referring back to the example of Bermondsey and Old Southwark. Imagine the Liberal Democrats lost support to both other parties. If the loss were bad enough, under the present rules, Hughes could lose to his Labour challenger but under the alternative vote it would be easier for him to survive, since the Conservative would be eliminated and some of the votes lost would return to Hughes as second preferences. As a result, the Day of Judgment might be a very poor instrument for removing a government of such candidates. Again, effective democracy would be damaged.

The case of the issues raised in Chapter 4 is more complicated. Some single-issue and sectional groups will not be favoured by the alternative vote because they will find it impossible to attract large numbers of second and subsequent preferences. However, this need not be true of all such parties. Were regionalist parties to become established, it is not clear whether the supporters of a major party would prefer the other major parties to the local parties. Such parties might offer an ideal way of *avoiding* supporting one of the other major parties. So the alternative vote certainly offers no guarantees against a proliferation of such parties.

With these things in mind we should note that the most curious thing about the advocacy of the alternative vote is how poorly it scores in serving the principled objectives of the advocates of proportional representation. It is not merely that it is not a proportional system: far from it. There is an even more powerful argument than that. It is that the alternative vote specifically stacks the deck *against* small parties with particular and possibly extreme views. The 'extreme' candidate is the one who will gain few second and subsequent preferences and will therefore be *less* well-placed than under the current system.

THE CASE AGAINST VOTING REFORM

The Electoral Reform Society (ERS) is now on the side of a 'yes' vote in the referendum, although it was once known as the Proportional Representation Society and has in the past disparaged the alternative vote. As recently as June 2009, its then Director, Ken Ritchie, said:

> at a time when our democratic institutions are in crisis, a move to AV would be nothing short of negligence … People are looking for choice and accountability at elections, with a vote that might actually count. That simply won't happen with AV.[19]

So it is surprising to find that now, the ERS not only proffers the same three reasons as 'Yes to Fairer Votes' in support of the alternative vote but also adds a further one – namely that the alternative vote 'penalises extremist parties'.[20] In other words, it is a movement *away* from proportionality.

Perhaps the fact that the alternative vote has the effect of damaging the prospects of extreme parties is a desirable one. It should be recalled that the same applies to any parties which do not attract second preferences, irrespective of whether they are usually regarded as extreme. The Scottish National Party is, in a sense, an extreme party, since it wishes independence for Scotland (it is therefore not quite like the regional parties I considered earlier). I do not know whether the supporters of other major parties would be likely or unlikely to put nationalists second. More importantly, there does not seem to be any reason why the answer to that question should be crucial in determining whether any nationalist MPs are elected – but it easily could be.

Another response relates to the *principle* of proportional representation. The basic appeal of that kind of system is clear: minority groups with a modicum of political organisation can achieve representation. The basis of the advocacy of the alternative vote is quite contrary: it is – supposedly – the mark of a good system that candidates with only a modicum of support should be quickly dismissed, and have their chances of election minimised. The argument is, in other words, entirely contrary to the principled case for proportional representation.

Despite the slipperiness of the Electoral Reform Society, the alternative vote seems to satisfy none of the basic requirements of the advocates of proportional representation – it is neither proportional nor promotes the representation of minorities. On the other hand, it does pose very much the same dangers to effective, realistic, functioning democracy as those systems.

Perhaps we should not be surprised by this. Indeed, perhaps it is a kind of omen that this dreadful system was proposed to us by a coalition of two parties which had – for a long time and quite rightly – opposed it.

CONCLUSION

Most of this book has been about why proportional representation is a bad idea. In Chapter 5, I turned to the alternative vote, which is not a proportional system at all. I suppose I could be accused of wasting the reader's time for 109 pages but it is hard to see what the case for the alternative vote is unless we take it either to be a pale version of proportional representation or possibly a step on the way to it. It seems that most of the people advocating a 'yes' vote are actually supporters of proportional representation and there is no doubt that the reason we are having a referendum at all is that the case for proportional representation has been made with some force ever since the 1970s.

As a final goal, the alternative vote offers nothing at all. It threatens us with the problems of coalition but gives

CONCLUSION

nothing in return. It is said to diminish the number of safe
seats but while it makes some seats less safe for a party, it
makes others safer. In any case, no seat is safe for an individual, as the fall-out from the expenses scandal shows. It
does not guarantee the election of a candidate who is preferred by most voters to each of the other candidates and
it does not put an end to tactical voting. If it does some of
the other things that it is said to, such as promote less antagonistic campaigning, only those who have not appreci-
ated the operation of the party system will welcome it. As
to proportionality, in circumstances like those which have
prevailed in the last few elections, it would surely give more
seats to the Liberal Democrats but probably do nothing
for other less than proportionally represented groups, and
might harm them. In circumstances different from those of
the last few elections, it might do any of a number of things,
some of which are dramatically less proportional than what
we are used to, including giving a Commons majority to
a party coming third in the national vote. How can these
things be thought 'fair'?

Perhaps the alternative vote is supposed to be merely
the first step and a renewed case for proportional representation will follow. If the alternative vote is implemented,
hung parliaments will be more likely, so another bargain,
over another referendum, might seem possible. The example of the apparently stalled, and certainly incomplete,

rolling reform of the House of Lords should warn against the view that adopting unsatisfactory interim proposals is a responsible way to proceed. More importantly, if that is the idea, then the case against proportional representation comes to the fore. There is nothing to be said for a bad system if it is merely a step on the way to another bad system.

The case for proportional representation, and the case for the alternative vote towed along behind, go wrong before they start. Their advocates make presumptions of which they seem to be unaware and they certainly never stop to consider where they might be leading. They think of one criterion of good democracy – 'fairness' – and one standard of 'fairness' – proportionality or something near it – in Parliament. They imagine this will somehow make for a government which is 'representative' and 'responsive' and that a new attitude of co-operation will infuse political debate. They imagine this will make our country 'more democratic' but think very little about what it is that makes democracy valuable, hardly anything of what it takes to make it work and even less about how different voting rules encourage different patterns of behaviour by the parties. It is as if all the harshness of the world can be washed away by watery-eyed visions of harmony.

The case *against* proportional representation is different. It starts with the question of what democracy is all about and the recognition that we face a choice about what kind of democracy to have. Before we make that choice, we should recognise that politics is a competition for leadership and, first and foremost, a competition for government. The voters are the judges in that competition. Political parties are, first and foremost, the vehicles in which politicians contest for power. Democracy, meanwhile, is always, and ever will be, an imperfect system. However well it works, it gives no guarantees of good or acceptable policy. In trying to make it work, we cannot ever assess voter preferences fully and we cannot ever give an unambiguously accurate translation of preferences into parliamentary representation. It is bound to be politicians, rather than saints, who make up our parliaments and we cannot ever quite trust them. Politicians will scheme for advantage; when things go wrong, they will try to shift blame and when they go right, claim credit. Each party will, on the whole, stick together, even when its members disagree. Certainly, they will not admit to an internal crisis. In government, they will not admit to mistakes, although when defeated they may feign humility. Of all the imperfections of democracy, perhaps the least noted is that the voters themselves are far from all-knowing. Most of us give political questions only limited attention; we do not work out all the intricacies of each manoeuvre and what it means and certainly we do not master the details of each policy proposal, much less of each manifesto. Yet all this is the material from which we must build a democracy. What is to be done?

There is a kind of democracy – the kind which seems to be the vision of the advocates of proportional representation – in which each organised group of voters can bid for parliamentary representation with a view to selling their votes for whatever they will fetch in support of one or other coalition. Such a system can be expected to gestate numerous little parties, each of which appeals – albeit possibly strongly – to only a small group of voters. Some of these parties will surely be brought forth into the world and can be expected to have a thoroughly divisive effect. In watered-down versions – still proclaiming 'fair votes' – we are asked to consider mechanisms which specifically subvert the principle of proportionality to ensure there are only a small number of parties. Once these devices for limiting representation in Parliament are introduced, the proposal is plainly neither one of proportional representation nor based on any general claim of fairness. Even in so far as it retains some part of the motivation of those plans, it sets up conditions to defeat its own objectives by different means. A Parliament with, say, three parties of significance, is precisely the one in which a third party is in the position of kingmaker and consequently can exert far more power than it has properly earned from voters' support. At least, in a truly multi-party system, there are alternative coalition partners, so no one party is so empowered.

Either version gives us only a very rudimentary fairness and the latter only partially gives us even that. And what democracy we lose in exchange! In these systems, the composition of government is determined by coalition agreement. This point is crucial, because it means that the composition of government is not determined by elections. The voters are the losers because they no longer choose their government. They choose their Parliament but the *government* is not formed in proportion to the voter's choices; rather, the party leaders decide who forms the government and the voters wait until they are told.

The quality of democracy is further harmed by the facts of coalition. In campaigns, parties and the wiser voters alike know that manifestos can only be negotiating positions. They might not even be honest versions of those but that is the most they can be. No one can really know what they are being offered. At the end of a coalition, they cannot even really know who is responsible for anything, so they cannot properly assess the parties in retrospect and must vote again blindfold, unable to see who has really done what; only speculating as to the seriousness of any new undertakings.

That is certainly bad enough but the quality of democracy and of government, and probably the fabric of society, are harmed still more when parties do not even aspire to forming a government alone. The art of politics becomes on the one hand that of mobilising small groups to elect cliques and on the other that of the cliques achieving agreement with other cliques to share power. In some cases, the trick must be to incite the voters to vote for a party just because it is *their* party; the party for people like them, the party for people who are different from the rest. In other cases, it might be to offer ever-inflated promises, with each disappointment blamed on the necessity of coalition. And with enough frustration at it all, in other cases, the trick might be to be the charismatic leader on a disguised ego trip.

In our current system, everything is different. Most of the time, when the votes are counted, we know what government we have. We must accept that it makes life hard for small parties and small swings in votes can bring large changes in seats. But these things are not 'unfairness', they are the magic of the system. It is because of these things that our elections can decide who governs. Still, we also have to accept that it is not a perfect system even in this limited objective. Sometimes coalition is unavoidable; sometimes there are ways of looking at a result that suggest we have the wrong government. But democracy will be imperfect. If elections imperfectly determine who governs, they still determine who governs. The central point is not that it should be perfect; the central point is that it is the voters, not the party leaders, who choose the government.

CONCLUSION

So let us be clear about these two *kinds* of democracy. In one, voters choose a Parliament and leave it to those in Parliament to determine who governs. In the other, voters decide who governs. There is not much point in trying to say that one of these is 'fairer' than the other and if we were to try to argue which is 'more democratic', I doubt we would get very far. But we might ask which we would prefer and before doing that we should consider what further consequences the current system has.

Encouraged to think that they can govern alone, our parties seek to win outright. They cannot possibly do that by appealing to a narrow group and instead they strain every sinew to widen their appeal. In the end, we need to have policies for the whole nation and we are much more likely to get them from parties seeking government than we are from parties seeking assured support from their particular group. We do not need new ideas from different parties, because good ideas will always have a place in the minds of those trying to win power. And we certainly do not need the parties to tell us how much they agree with each other, because if we are to judge the ideas they advance, we need to hear *two* sides. On each of these issues, the system induces the parties to behave in a way that empowers the voters, and to form policies, as best they can, to achieve broad support.

Once we have a government, there are further benefits. Our government still depends on us, because the Day of

Judgment will come. We know what we have been promised and are expecting and we know what we are assessing when the next election comes. If on that Day the government loses the support of the voters, it cannot rearrange the coalition and carry on. It must just pack up and go. Not only can governments never escape the Day of Judgment, they can never forget it. And during a parliament, parties try to please electors not only with promises but with actions. Thus democracy, properly organised, properly functioning, controls its leaders.

With the opposition ever-critical, ever-hungry, the Day of Judgment is ever-present in the minds of our leaders. The election must be won or everything is ended: all power, all prestige – all gone. The Day of Judgment is the means by which the proud fall, and the haughty are deposed. It makes the powerful meek, servants out of masters and supplicants out of rulers. And the Day of Judgment is *ours*. It gives *power* to the people. Long live democracy!

APPENDIX
VOTING SYSTEMS

The current British voting system is sometimes called 'first past the post', although that is a little misleading, since there is no 'post' towards which the candidates are racing. In this system, each constituency elects one MP. Voters mark the candidate they support and the one with the most votes wins.

The 'alternative vote' system is the subject of the referendum. In this system voters have the option of expressing a number of preferences. They vote by ranking the candidates first, second, third and so on, for as many choices as they wish. Initially, the number of first preferences for each candidate is counted. If any one has more than half, he or she is elected. If not, the candidate with fewest votes is eliminated and the second preferences (if any) of those who voted for the eliminated candidate are counted and added to the scores of the remaining candidates. Another check is made to see whether any candidate has more votes than all the others together. If so, that candidate is elected; if not, the bottom candidate is again eliminated. The process continues until one candidate has more votes than the total of all those remaining put together. That candidate is then elected.

In both first past the post and the alternative vote, the House of Commons is made up of the winners from each constituency. Systems of proportional representation are rather different and aim at achieving a close relationship between the proportion of votes for each party and the proportion of seats it takes in Parliament. The extent to which they achieve this is very variable and depends on the details of the system. However, at least as far as the larger parties are concerned, they will normally result in more proportional outcomes than either first past the post or the alternative vote.

There are hundreds of systems of proportional representation systems but we can distinguish three broad families. One involves constituencies with more than one MP. It could be as few as two or three or it could be many more. The larger the number of members for each constituency, the better the approximation to proportionality. The so-called 'single transferable vote' (STV) system is of this family. In this variant, there will typically be more than one candidate from each party and voters can express preferences between candidates of the same party as well as between parties. British advocates of STV envisage constituencies of around five to eight members. If there were only three parties, with six or seven member constituencies STV would normally achieve a high degree of proportionality but when there are a larger number of parties, this will not be true.

The second broad family is the 'additional member system'. In this, constituencies elect a single MP, either by first past the post or the alternative vote. Since this offers no guarantee of proportionality, additional MPs, without constituencies – 'top-up MPs' as they are sometimes called – are added, to bring the total numbers towards proportionality. The degree of proportionality usually depends on how many top-up MPs there are and there is a multitude of ways of calculating how many each party should have. Most suggestions are that top-up MPs should make up somewhere between fifteen and fifty per cent of the total. At the lower end, there would be no guarantee of proportionality, particularly for smaller parties.

Third is the 'party list' system. In this system, voters simply vote for the party of their choice. The total votes for each party across the whole country are counted and seats in Parliament allocated in proportion to the votes. The particular individuals who become the MPs are nominated by the parties and there are no constituencies. This actually achieves proportional representation.

NOTES

Introduction

1. *Independent* 22 April 2010
2. A very abstract one is Michael Dummett (1997) *Principles of electoral reform*. Oxford: OUP. Another which gives much more attention to the realities of British politics is Alan Renwick (2011) *A citizen's guide to electoral reform*. London: Biteback. Neither of these gives much attention to the issues I suggest are important but they give a balanced treatment of the various systems on the terms of the arguments as they are normally made.
3. S E Finer (1975) *Adversary politics and electoral reform*. London: Anthony Wigram.
4. Jenkins Commission (1998) *The Report of the Independent Commission on the Voting System (The Jenkins Commission)*. London: The Stationery Office.

NOTES

Chapter 1

1. *Daily Telegraph* 16 April 2010.
2. *Guardian* 16 April 2010.
3. *The Times* 16 April 2010.
4. Joseph Schumpeter (1943) *Capitalism, socialism and democracy*. London: George Allen & Unwin.
5. Karl Popper (1944) *The open society and its enemies, part 1: Plato*. Princeton: Princeton University Press, p. 124.
6. An issue explored in Michael Foley (2000) *The British Presidency*. Manchester: Manchester University Press, and Graham Allen (2003) *The last Prime Minister*. Thorverton: Imprint Academic.
7. Enid Lakeman (1982) *Power to elect*. London: Heinemann/ Electoral Reform Society, p. 164, noted that the Socialist government elected in France was committed to 21 specific measures and said that, had they been blessed with STV, French voters could have secured a majority in Parliament only for those of the 21 that a majority favoured.

Chapter 2

1. Author's calculations from data from news.bbc.co.uk/1/ shared/election2010/results/.
2. www.bbc.co.uk/news/magazine-11400138.
3. Many scholars, starting with Christopher Robson and Brendan Walsh (1973) 'The importance of positional voting bias in the Irish General Election of 1973', *Political Studies*

pp. 191–203, have found evidence that candidates' positions on the ballot paper affect how many votes they win.

4. There is a good collection in Peter C Fishburn (1974) 'Paradoxes of voting', *American Political Science Review* pp. 537–546.

5. www.bbc.co.uk/news/uk-politics-11387935.

6. Enid Lakeman (1982) *Power to elect*. London: Heinemann/ Electoral Reform Society, p. 165.

7. Michael Pinto-Duschinsky (1999) 'Send the rascals packing', *Representation* pp. 117–126. (Reprinted from the *Times Literary Supplement*, 25 September 1998).

8. Philip Cowley (2005) *The rebels: how Blair mislaid his majority*. London: Methuen.

Chapter 3

1. Nouriel Roubini and Jeffrey Sachs (1989) 'Political and economic determinants of budget deficits in the industrial democracies', *European Economic Review* pp. 903–938.

2. www.bbc.co.uk/news/uk-politics-11570593.

3. news.bbc.co.uk/1/hi/uk_politics/election_2010/8607698. stm and www.bbc.co.uk/news/uk-politics-11532321.

4. Edmund Burke (1770) *Thoughts on the present discontents*.

5. Again, I am arguing along the lines of Joseph Schumpeter (1943) *Capitalism, socialism and democracy*. London: George Allen & Unwin.

6. Tony Blair (2010) *A journey*. London: Hutchinson, p. 84.

7. Ibid., p. 94.

NOTES

8. A video can be seen at www.thesun.co.uk/sol/homepage/ news/3157502/David-Miliband-sees-Red-Ed-mist-with-Harriet-Harman-over-Iraq-War.html.

9. The argument was first notably analysed by Duncan Black (1948) 'On the rationale of group decision-making', *Journal of Political Economy* pp. 23–34. It is an application of something sometimes called 'the median voter theorem'.

10. Even Danny Alexander, formerly Director of Communications for Britain in Europe, now a Liberal Democrat member of the government, has fallen into line with public opinion: www.bbc.co.uk/news/uk-politics-11380431. Ken Clarke did so, for all practical purposes, a little earlier: news.bbc.co.uk/1/hi/uk_politics/7837116.stm.

11. It featured in their manifestos of 1992, 1997 and 2001, sometimes being described as a 'flagship' policy.

12. Jan de Meyer (1983) 'Coalition government in Belgium' in *Coalition government in western Europe*, Vernon Bogdanor (Ed.) London: Policy Studies Institute/Heinemann, p. 198.

13. Jan Vis (1983) 'Coalition government in a constitutional monarchy: The Dutch experience' in *Coalition government in Western Europe*, Vernon Bogdanor (Ed.) London: Policy Studies Institute/Heinemann, p. 155.

14. Michael Pinto-Duschinsky (1998) 'Send the rascals packing', *Representation*, pp. 117–126. (Reprinted from the *Times Literary Supplement*, 25 September 1998 p. 120).

15. www.bbc.co.uk/news/uk-politics-11851318.

16. www.bbc.co.uk/news/uk-politics-11803719.

17. *People* 25 April 2010.

Chapter 4

1. www.irishtimes.com/newspaper/ireland/2010/0205/
   1224263814106.html.

2. Jenkins Commission (1998) *The Report of the Independent
   Commission on the Voting System (The Jenkins Commission)*. London:
   The Stationery Office, para 92.

3. Vernon Bogdanor (1983) 'Reflections on coalition
   government', *Policy Studies* pp. 50–64, 61.

4. nus.org.uk/en/News/News/1500-candidates-across-97-of-
   constituencies-sign-pledge-to-oppose-higher-tuition-fees/.

5. www.timesonline.co.uk/tol/news/politics/article7124090.
   ece part 8.

6. Allan Gibbard (1973) 'Manipulation of voting schemes: a
   general result', *Econometrica* pp. 587–601.

7. Vernon Bogdanor (1983) (Ed.) *Coalition government in western
   Europe*, London Policy Studies Institute/Heinemann pp. 8–9.

8. Jenkins Commission (1998) *The Report of the Independent
   Commission on the Voting System (The Jenkins Commission)*. London:
   The Stationery Office, paras 145–150.

9. My calculations are based on data from news.bbc.co.uk/1/
   shared/bsp/hi/elections/euro/09/html/ukregion_999999.
   stm.

10. General Election results from news.bbc.co.uk/1/shared/
    election2010/results.

11. Jenkins Commission (1998) *The Report of the Independent
    Commission on the Voting System (The Jenkins Commission)*. London:
    The Stationery Office, para 144.

12. An example used to make this point by Sir Leslie Stephen (1882) *Science of ethics*. London: Smith, Elder & Co., p. 143.
13. www.scottish.parliament.uk/business/research/briefings-03/sb03–25.pdf, p. 3.
14. www.humberbridge.co.uk/media/reports/HBBManReport2009.pdf.
15. www.voteenglish.org/stop-paying-scotland/.
16. Maurice Duverger (1954) *Political parties*. London: Methven & Co. Ltd.
17. Ibid., p. 284.
18. Ibid., p. 285.
19. *Guardian* 13 November 2010.
20. www.bbc.co.uk/news/uk-politics-11473609.
21. www.bbc.co.uk/news/uk-politics-11473609.
22. *Daily Telegraph* 10 October 2010.

Chapter 5

1. Enid Lakeman (1974) *How democracies vote*. London: Faber and Faber Limited, p. 67.
2. S E Finer (1975) *Adversary politics and electoral reform*. London: Anthony Wigram, p. 23.
3. The Hansard Society is a charity, which commissioned a panel of notable figures, chaired by Lord Blake, to produce an authoritative report on voting systems. Hansard Society (1976) *The Report of the Hansard Society Commission on Electoral Reform*. London: The Hansard Society for Parliamentary Government, para 82.

NOTES

4. Jenkins Commission (1998) *The Report of the Independent Commission on the Voting System (The Jenkins Commission)*. London: The Stationery Office, para 82.

5. Vernon Bogdanor (1983) 'Introduction' in *Democracy and elections*, Vernon Bogdanor and David Butler (Eds), Cambridge: CUP, p. 5.

6. This way of looking at it was considered by Michael Dummett (1997) *Principles of electoral reform*. Oxford: OUP.

7. 'Note of reservation by Lord Alexander' in *Report of the Independent Commission on the Voting System (The Jenkins Commission)*, London: The Stationery Office, p. 55.

8. news.smh.com.au/breaking-news-national/poll-shows-support-for-electoral-reform-20101015-16mks.html. Australian election results at http://www.aph.gov.au/library/pubs/rb/2004–05/05RB11-1e.htm

9. Patrick Dunleavy, Helen Margetts, B O'Duffy and Stuart Weir (1997) 'Remodelling the 1997 General Election: How Britain would have voted under alternative electoral systems', *Journal of elections, public opinions and parties* pp. 208–231.

10. Peter Kellner *Submission to the independent commission on the voting system*, para 4.15c. In *Report of the Independent Commission on the Voting System (The Jenkins Commission), Volume 2*, London: The Stationery Office.

11. David Butler (1998) 'Report of group of academics chaired by Professor David Butler, Nuffield College, Oxford' in *Report of the Independent Commission on the voting system (The Jenkins Commission), Volume 2*, London: The Stationery Office, p. 11.

NOTES

12. *New Statesman* 5 November 2009.

13. www.guardian.co.uk/politics/2010/nov/16/labour-liberal-democrats-grassroots-alliance.

14. R M Punnett (1991) 'The alternative vote re-visited', *Electoral Studies* pp. 281–289.

15. www.guardian.co.uk/news/datablog/2010/may/07/uk-election-results-data-candidates-seats#data.

16. www.timesonline.co.uk/tol/news/politics/article6350604. ece.

17. www.dailymail.co.uk/news/election/article-1274495/UK-ELECTION-RESULTS-2010-Jacqui-Smith-expenses-scandal-MPs-lose-seats.html.

18. Such as Michael Dummett (1997) *Principles of electoral reform*. Oxford: OUP.

19. www.electoral-reform.org.uk/news.php?ex=0&nid=368.

20. www.electoral-reform.org.uk/article.php?id=55.

INDEX

INDEX

INDEX

INDEX